THE PELICAN LATIN AMERICAN LIBRARY

*General Editor: Richard Gott*

Peasant Rebellion in Latin America

Gerrit Huizer studied social psychology at Amsterdam University, and has been active in community development and peasant organization since 1955. He worked to begin with as a volunteer in a village in Central America, and later in villages in Sicily in a project directed by Danilo Dolci. From 1962 to 1971 he worked in several capacities with different agencies of the United Nations (particularly I.L.O.) in Latin America and South-East Asia, concentrating mainly on field-projects and action research. He has written a considerable number of articles about these experiences for literary and professional journals in the Netherlands, Latin America and the U.S.A. *Peasant Rebellion in Latin America* is a considerably abridged version of his Ph.D. dissertation, which came out as *The Revolutionary Potential of Peasants in Latin America* (Lexington, Mass.: Heath Lexington Books, 1972). Since 1971 Gerrit Huizer has been visiting professor at the Institute of Social Studies in The Hague and research fellow at the Institute for Development Research in Copenhagen.

D1150337

*Gerrit Huizer*

# Peasant Rebellion in Latin America

The Origins, Forms of Expression, and
Potential of Latin American
Peasant Unrest

 Penguin Books

Penguin Books Ltd, Harmondsworth,
Middlesex, England
Penguin Books Australia Ltd, Ringwood,
Victoria, Australia

First published 1973

Made and printed in Great Britain by
Hazell Watson & Viney Ltd,
Aylesbury, Bucks
Set in Linotype Juliana

# Contents

# Introduction

This book has grown over the past fifteen years as a result of involvement in development work in several countries of the Third World, chiefly in Latin America. This explains why the main bias behind this study is the desire to find practical and feasible solutions for the problems that the peasants face in most countries of the Third World.

The great majority of these peasants are dominated and exploited by a relatively small class of large landowners. The United Nations and other international agencies have indicated that this situation is a major obstacle to the social and economic development of the countries of the Third World, particularly in Latin America. The landowning elites usually spend their considerable earnings conspicuously and in ways highly detrimental to the national economies, rather than in a manner that would stimulate development. Only a radical change in the large-estate system would free the economic resources currently monopolized for personal consumption by this small privileged group. Such a change would, at the same time, free the energies of the peasants to participate in a national development effort that would give them a just share in the benefits.

In many countries, plans have been made and laws have been promulgated in order to bring about this needed radical change in the traditional estate system that has been so frequently recommended by the United Nations. But in most cases the results have been highly disappointing.

In the meantime, the past decade has seen the appearance of a whole literature devoted to the lack of success of development programmes and projects undertaken in the context of traditionally structured societies. The passive reaction of the peasantry to these development efforts has given the impression that the traditional 'peasant sub-culture', or peasant mentality, is a main obstacle to development. On the surface this explanation seems appropriate, but once one gets more profoundly involved in peasant life, and in efforts to stimulate peasants towards new responsibilities, it proves to be erroneous.

'Resistance to change' by the peasant is mainly a reaction of self-defence against the 'resistance to change' of the traditional elites which fear to lose their domination over the peasants. It appears that peasants can be mobilized quite well if the purpose of the mobilization is to change the existing *status quo* for a system under which the peasants can reasonably expect effective improvements. This discovery and its consequences for action constitute the main theme of this book. The way the discovery was made has been highly empirical and practical, often through some kind of involvement in the life of the peasants.

In the first chapter it will be shown that peasant distrust and 'resistance to change' in Latin America, rather than being a symptom of a natural or traditional incapacity and unwillingness to change, can best be explained as the result of a prolonged period of repression. Peasant resistance in the past to the introduction of the large-estate (*hacienda*) system was violently crushed, but it continued to spring up again on numerous occasions. Only through the exercise of overt or covert repression of the peasantry was the *hacienda* system able to establish and maintain itself, creating for the peasants living under its sphere of influence what has been called the 'culture of repression' or 'internal colonialism'.

In the second and third chapters two cases are described where 'resistance to change' and distrust on the part of the peasants have been encountered as an obstacle to the usual kind of community development efforts. In these cases, through personal involvement in their life and problems it was possible to study the implications of the peasants' distrust.

Gradually, through some experiences with factors related to this distrust, I was able to discover the good reasons behind it, and to see that the distrust could in fact be turned into a mobilizing force for social change. The first field experience described here took place in 1955, when I spent almost a year in a small village in El Salvador doing community development field work. In the effort to implement some community improvement projects it was found that the distrust of the peasants, and their initial refusal to participate in the project, was related to the fact that they lived under the *hacienda* system in a 'culture of repression'. Their distrust proved to be justified. Changes were introduced into the village only piecemeal, and opportunities for more substantial change were purposely blocked by the landowners and the government agencies controlled by them.

But an experiment carried out on another occasion, during a year of community development work in the Punitaqui area in Chile in 1965–6, gave clear proof of how peasant distrust and 'resistance to change' could be turned into well-organized peasant action. Once peasant attention was focused, and after initial efforts had been directed against the forces of landlord control and were clearly shown to be to the benefit of the peasants, enthusiastic participation resulted.

Experience there showed that peasant distrust can be one of the most important promoters of change and development if it is used as a force that brings peasants together in a common struggle in opposition to the traditional vested interests of landlords and other repressive forces. The growth of several strong peasant organizations that have been crucial in the promotion of radical change in some Latin American countries was one result of these forces, as is described in Chapters 4 and 5.

The organizations dealt with are the agrarian movements in Mexico, Bolivia and Venezuela. Others are the regional peasant organizations in Peru (particularly in the valley of La Convención and in the central highlands) and the Peasant Leagues in the north-east of Brazil. The violence occurring in Colombia and Guatemala, as a result of the manner in which the traditional elite tried to maintain the *status quo*, will also be described briefly, since it, too, appears to have had a radicalizing effect on the peasantry.

Chapter 6 deals with the questions *where, when,* and *how* effective peasant organizations can be created. In addition to overall peasant distrust and resentment, a number of specific conditions exist which seem to make a peasant organization a practicable proposition. These are the factors that nearly all the large-scale peasant organizations looked at here have in common : modernizing influences that bring frustration rather than real improvements to the peasants, and closeness to urban areas which enhances the chance of the appearance of able leadership from within, or support from outside. The actual formation of peasant organizations has been started most fruitfully where acute grievances exist of which the peasants have a keen awareness. The availability of charismatic and incorruptible leadership is essential to bring the peasants to united action regarding those grievances and frustrations. To become effective at a later stage, support is needed from urban allies who can help to establish a region-wide organizational structure.

The best way to utilize peasant distrust as a positive force is to engage the peasants in a struggle through organized action for their most basic demand : land. The approach used in response to the increasingly violent reactions of the large landowners against the growing peasant movements is the escalation of demands and tactics of the struggle. How this has been done by most existing organizations is described in the last part of Chapter 6.

Finally, in Chapter 7, the effect of the peasant movements as a political force is evaluated, particular emphasis being given to the possibilities for future radical or revolutionary peasant action. Practically all situations existing at present in Latin America contain considerable revolutionary potential :

1. straightforwardly repressive regimes maintaining the *status quo* are increasingly considered to be illegitimate;

2. regimes that have neutralized a strongly organized peasantry are creating new frustrations;

3. 'populist' regimes that try to introduce change but are not radical enough to satisfy basic peasant demands are creating uncertainty and high expectations with an explosive effect.

The overall presence of distrust and resentment among peasants under the traditional *hacienda* system, in addition to the frustrating effects of modernization, seem to make the peasants ready for militant organization as soon as they can find sympathetic and able allies to guide and support them.

# CHAPTER 1

# The Background to
# Peasant Distrust
# in Latin America

The present situation in Latin America, and the potential for organizing the peasantry, have to be seen in the perspective of historical development. The colonial period brought forms of social organization to Latin America which still persist in many areas today. Although there is considerable variation from country to country, and from region to region, on the whole the social system in rural Latin America is characterized by the latifundia or the *hacienda* (*fazenda* in Brazil) system. The fertile valleys or coastal lowlands, cultivated during the pre-colonial civilizations by the indigenous groups, were transformed into large estates belonging to the conquerors and their heirs. In some areas they were used for pasture, elsewhere for plantation agriculture. The indigenous peasants were in part sent as cheap labour to the mines, in which the conquerors were chiefly interested, or, if they did not want to work on the estates, they were driven into subsistence agriculture on the mountain slopes. Once a certain equilibrium had been established by armed force, legal provisions were made in several countries to give the indigenous population minimum guarantees for survival. Regulations were issued which protected the remaining indigenous *comunidades* from complete extinction. Several cases are known where recourse to such legal protection was made in vain and where the peasants took up arms to defend their rights against usurpations. Such self-defence activities were

normally countered by the armed forces of the landowners
or the national army, and smothered in blood. But sometimes
they reached such proportions that regional or nation-wide
protest movements developed into a kind of internal war.
The movement led by the Indian leader Túpac Amaru in the
Andean highlands at the end of the eighteenth century is a
case in point.

After the end of the colonial epoch, the local white or
*mestizo* elite in most of the Latin American countries expanded its wealth and power in an aggressive way, mainly
at the cost of the indigenous peasants. Thus was initiated
the process of pushing back the indigenous peasant population towards more remote and even more barren agricultural
areas. Though the peasants frequently tried to defend their
land, most of the resistance movements, being scattered and
organized on only a small scale, were bloodily repressed. Few
of these rebellions became widespread and made a considerable national impact: one such was the peasant movement
led by Zarate Willka in 1898-9 in the Bolivian highlands,
which helped a Liberal government come to power. However, after the change of regime the promises of justice to
the indigenous peasants were forgotten, the leader Willka
was assassinated, and the peasant armies were overcome by
the government's army.

On the whole it is clear that the hacienda system of the
rural areas of most of Latin America was established in
circumvention of traditional law and of the rules of fair play.
For that reason the legitimacy of the new structure, the
latifundia-minifundia complex, has remained permanently in
question. In several countries lawsuits concerning land have
been going on for many decades. Most were lost by the
peasant communities because they lacked funds for paying
lawyers and the other costs involved in the suit, and such
cases were decided automatically in favour of the large proprietors. Resentment and a strong feeling of injustice re-

mained with the peasants, who had become serfs or workers on their former lands. Outwardly, however, they conformed to the newly established order.

There is considerable variety in the peasants' conditions of work on the estates in the different countries. A system of servitude or semi-servitude was imposed, called *huasipungo* in Ecuador, *colonato* in Bolivia and Central America, *yana-conaje* in Peru, *inquilinaje* in Chile and *cambão* in Brazil. In exchange for the right to use a small subsistence plot, the peasants were obliged to work a number of days each week without pay on the land of the owner. The obligatory work consisted mainly of normal agricultural tasks, but in many areas it included all kinds of services in the homes of the estate owners both in town and on the estate. Usually in some countries in former days, and occasionally today, daughters had to be provided for the sexual pleasures of the landlord. In areas where the role of the *patrón* and of the peasants on his estate are well defined by tradition and have functioned for a long time there is little open resistance from the peasants. But the system easily lends itself to abuse, and such instances cause a great deal of resentment. To check such resentment, and prevent it from developing into open resistance, the *status quo* is maintained by severe sanctions. Minor errors or offences by peasants are punished disproportionately. The peasantry has thus been kept in a state of constant fear under a permanent threat of violence, creating a climate which the anthropologist Holmberg defined as a 'culture of repression'.

The fears mentioned by Holmberg as being most strikingly present among the peasants were: fear of death by capital punishment, fear of the pain of corporal punishment, fear of incarceration, fear of the landlord's disapproval, fear of the loss of property, fear of hunger, and fear of the supernatural. It was noted that the behaviour of the serf peasants was often defined by the strongest of competing fears. A peasant whose animal was taken away by the estate owner would not complain, since fear of patronal disapproval or even of incarceration was stronger than fear of the loss of property, or of hunger. The whole complex of complementary or, at times, competing fears makes the peasants seek to avoid any danger and risk involved in contact with outsiders and new situations. The 'culture of repression' reinforces itself through these fears, and makes the introduction of changes extremely difficult.

The situation in which the peasantry lives, both free peasants and those on haciendas, has also been called 'internal colonialism'.* This phenomenon arose as a result of the expansion of the capitalist economy during the second half of the nineteenth century, accompanied by the ideology of economic liberalism, as a new form of colonialism. That the situation of 'internal colonialism' was never completely accepted is clear from the way the hacienda owners felt they had to repress or terrorize the peasants of their estates or of surrounding communities. It is understandable under these circumstances that wherever community development projects and smiliar efforts are promoted by agencies of a government that is controlled by the traditional elite the peasants will show distrust and 'resistance to change'.

A great deal of literature exists on the 'resistance to change' of the peasants. If one takes into account the ample descriptions of the existence and frequency of 'resistance to change', and related phenomena in traditional communities, one might be inclined to see development and organizational efforts in the rural areas as a hopeless undertaking. Only a

* Rodolfo Stavenhagen, 'Clases, Colonialismo y Aculturación', *América Latina*, VI, No. 4, Rio de Janeiro, 1963, p. 93; for a discussion of the term 'internal colonialism', increasingly used by scholars of various countries (such as René Dumont, C. Wright Mills), see Pablo Gonzalez Casanova, 'Sociedad Plural, Colonialismo Interno y Desarrollo', *América Latina*, vi, No. 3, Rio de Janeiro, 1963, pp. 15–32.

few scholars seem to have studied these phenomena and at the same time tried to overcome their impact in a pragmatic way. This is probably due to the bias among many social scientists that action disturbs a scientific and 'objective' view.

Some observers give the impression that characteristics such as distrust, lack of innovative spirit, fatalism, family-orientedness, dependence on government and lack of cosmopolitan orientation are part of a generalized 'sub-culture of peasantry'. However, it seems that there is not a characteristic and generalized 'peasant mentality' which is basically different from the mentality of other people. Peasants are 'apathetic' or 'organizable' according to circumstance, which, in the rural areas of Latin America, is determined by the prevailing 'culture of repression'.

CHAPTER 2

# A Field Experience in Central America: The Rationality of Distrust

That peasant distrust is not merely a negative reaction to development efforts but is related to a justified resentment towards the overall repressive system under which peasants live was studied at first hand during an experiment in peasant organization that I was able to carry out in a Central American village. During that experiment it could be seen that distrust was the main motivation for the peasants' lack of participation in community improvement efforts. This distrust could be overcome through the application of the community development approach, winning the peasants' confidence. However, the representatives of the predominant social system, the officials in the service of a government dominated by the large hacienda owners, proved to be unwilling to apply consistently these community development techniques, which are designed to stimulate active peasant participation. They blocked the experiment that was carried out, thus confirming how justified the peasants were in their distrust and in their feeling that minor changes did not mean a real and significant improvement in their situation.

Thanks to a UNESCO scholarship, I spent the year of 1955 as part of a team of volunteers assisting the Administración del Valle de la Esperanza in El Salvador in its community development efforts. This regional development agency of the Salvadorean government had already been working for some years in the region, concerned mainly with reconstruction and development made necessary by a severe earthquake in 1951.

One of the projects in which the volunteers assisted the Administración was to start a sanitation programme in a small village, San Luis, with the active participation of the villagers. The project involved the construction of a drinking water pipeline of several kilometres from a well in the mountains to the centre of the village. Previously the people had used contaminated water drawn from wells in the nearby riverbed. At a public meeting called by one of the directors of the Administración, the villagers had more or less agreed to do the manual labour, while the Administración was to contribute the pipes and other equipment and technical supervision. However, when the project was initiated the villagers did not actually take up their assigned work. This puzzled both the Administración and the voluntary team. When visits to the village made by the team to convince the population did not change this reluctance to work, it was decided that I should go and live in San Luis permanently, in order to find the reasons for this attitude and possibly help get the project under way.

It was quite obvious that one of the first things I had to do when going to live in San Luis was to win the confidence of the people. The fact that I was a foreigner (not placed socially), and especially the fact that I went to live in a hut like that of everybody else in the village (something Salvadorean upper- and middle-class people generally do not do), helped to gain the confidence of my neighbours. I relied mostly on the common human sympathy I felt for the villagers, using the following approach.

(1) It was essential to accept the people as they were, and not to take an educator's attitude. So I enjoyed being taught about local practices in many fields. I very seldom criticized their 'primitive' (as they called it themselves) way of life, and I was always eager to find something to admire, for

instance when I visited their houses. Even my lack of fluent Spanish in the beginning was a help.

(2) I shared, first passively and gradually more actively, the community life: sitting together with the men in the centre of the village or with one of the families at home, playing the guitar and singing, telling stories or listening to the local musicians and storytellers. I also participated in fiestas, funerals, hunting parties, and so on, so that the villagers got the feeling, and started to say, 'He belongs to us.'

(3) I shared the simple meals of a neighbour family, especially during the first weeks, and insisted on eating the same things in order to learn about their eating habits.

(4) Contrary to the habits of most local government officials, I kept every promise or appointment, and if this was impossible I explained carefully why, and apologized. Also contrary to what was usual, I never carried any weapon except the *machete*, big knife, that the peasants themselves use, and I always addressed the villagers with the polite form *Usted* unless I knew them very intimately, while government agents generally use *tu*.

The village of San Luis consisted of seventy-eight cottages, mostly straw huts and, for the rest, mud-walled houses, spread along a dirt road where only jeeps could pass in the dry season. This road connected the village with two small towns, in one of which the headquarters of the Administración del Valle de la Esperanza was established. There were seventy-eight families, seventy of which were classified as 'poor' by the Administración. The families that were not poor owned some land (five hectares or a little less) that was just enough for subsistence farming. However, even these families all had income from other sources, such as a son or unmarried brother working in some kind of job in one of the nearby small towns. The seventy families classified as 'poor' had very little land or none at all, and were dependent for the

most part on income earned from work as agricultural or
unskilled manual labourers.

Most of the land in the village belonged to one hacienda.
The owner lived most of the time in San Salvador, the capital
of the country. His land was very extensively cultivated.
Most of it was rather hilly, and used for grazing. In general,
the hacienda did not provide much work for the villagers, so
most of the men were obliged to look for work elsewhere.
They usually went as seasonal workers to the coffee plantations outside the area or to the construction sites of the
Administración in the surrounding towns (where practically
half of the houses had been destroyed during the 1951 earthquake). In San Luis there was little overt hostility towards
the local landlord. People did resent, however, that he did not
take care to exploit his lands better, so that they would have
more work.

Apart from the contrast between the world of the landlord
and that of the rest of the villagers, there was not much
differentiation or social stratification among the peasants of
San Luis. Although some of them had enough land to support themselves more or less independently, and most of
them had little or no land at all, they all felt strongly that
they lived in the same poverty.

From the first days of my participation in village life it was
quite clear that the main quality of life in San Luis for the
peasant class was suffering or, as the people themselves called
it, *tristeza*. Both the villagers and the officials of the Administración expressed amazement that I should care to share
this kind of life for some time.

After a few weeks when I began to feel that I was accepted
within the community, I started to try to find out the reason
for the people's negative reaction to the promises of the
government officials. This could be done in many personal
talks, especially in the evenings, when most of the men came
together to relax in the centre of the village. I soon discovered

that they suspected that the water-system would, in the end, lead, not up to the village for the benefit of everybody, but to the hacienda. Although the speeches of the officials inclined them to believe and hope for the best, they had been disappointed so often that in spite of some initial enthusiasm they maintained their distrust. The existing resentment expressed itelf in all kinds of statements that I either heard or overheard. The main tendency of these arguments with regard to the voluntary work can best be expressed more or less in the words of the villagers. They would say :

'Why are officials of the Administración earning twenty times as much as we do and telling us to work for nothing?'

'The government obviously has lots of money. Look at the wages of senior officials, cars and trucks running around all the time. See all the construction that is taking place in the towns, etc. When they don't want to pay us our modest wage, certainly somebody is filling his pockets with part of the money that is supposed to go for this (sanitation) project.'

'It isn't true that we can afford to do voluntary work because we are often unemployed. We need to hang around in case some odd job comes up somewhere.'

'You cannot work if you don't earn money for food. How can government officials know that working with an empty stomach is bad for your health and increases the risk of becoming sick, which would be disastrous in our conditions?'*

'Why should we pay taxes on the small piece of land or the ox-cart we happen to have, and besides that, work for nothing in order to have the government bring some improvement to our village?'

In addition, it was well known to the villagers that most of the higher officials of the Administración were either large

* Agricultural workers habitually get, besides their wages of ¢1.25 (0.80 dollar cents) a day, a meal consisting of *tortillas* and some beans; workers in government constructions get ¢2.00, and no such meals.

landholders themselves or related to them through family ties. Government officials who came to the villages for agricultural extension or community development activities were always armed with a pistol, a factor which did not contribute to winning the people's confidence, and which only emphasized the rigidity and potential instability of the rural power structure. Since the peasants could not openly disagree with or protest against the government officials, they feigned agreement with what was proposed but expressed their opposition by not showing up to do the voluntary work. In addition to this passive refusal to collaborate there was the simple fact of undernourishment, from which many peasants suffered between the coffee harvest seasons. This resulted in a half-conscious economizing of physical energy, and feelings of insecurity and apathy.

Some of the psychological factors related to undernourishment, which clearly formed a barrier to cooperation, were the feelings of powerlessness and inferiority that accompanied it. The obsession with a 'screaming stomach', completely occupied in getting fed, may explain why the villagers said that they lived 'just like animals'.

It was not only undernourishment that made people feel inferior and incapable of real self-help. The detrimental effect of unemployment on people's self-esteem should not be underestimated. They spent most of the year just idly waiting, in the hope that somehow somebody would give them work, and this had a considerable impact on their personalities. An additional aggravation was the fact that they had to take whatever came up. They had no rights at all, since there were so many people available who could take a job if they did not do so. These facts created strong feelings of hostility, towards the better-off classes and towards society as a whole. This form of aggression that was turned inward was one of the reasons for much of the drunkenness for which the area was ill famed. The most distressing fact was that the people themselves knew so well the impact of the three above-mentioned factors, and other problems, on their lives.

From the intimate reactions of people it became quite obvious that under a surface of apathy, indifference and distrust a strong resentment, if not hatred, existed, directed against the powerful, creating a climate of slumbering explosiveness. Government officials often warned me about the 'dangers' of living among the peasants.

Peasant unrest had existed in El Salvador ever since the creation of the large latifundia, but it became particularly strong after the Liberal government (1881–2) promulgated decrees extinguishing communities and *ejidos*. In 1885 and 1898 resistance movements sprang up against the despoliations. In the latter movement judges who had been helpful in dividing the lands of the villages were severely punished by having their hands cut off. The most violent reaction was the uprising of 1932, in which more than 60,000 peasants with primitive weapons revolted against the prevailing system. In the few days following, a great number were killed. Leftist political groups claimed that there were 30,000 people dead; the government said that there were 'only fifteen thousand'.

Many years after this massacre the rural areas were still under severe control by the Guardia Nacional. It often happened that quiet social gatherings of the peasants were broken up when the arrival in the neighbourhood of a police patrol, generally three heavily armed men, was announced. In the rural areas it was forbidden by law for more than five persons to gather in one place. The formation of peasant associations was also prohibited.

In this general climate the distrust of the peasants seemed rational and justified. Their passive refusal to participate in a project proposed by representatives of a government related to the landholding class could be seen as a logical response.

Not showing up at work when expected was the peasants' only way of affirming themselves and of saying 'no' to a society in which they had very little stake. People were partly aware of this themselves. Nevertheless, after living among the villagers for some months, I found it not difficult to persuade them to see how far they could benefit from the services the government offered. Voluntary work on the sanitation project, and later on the improvement of the road connecting the village with the nearby town, was undertaken, and was carried out with some degree of enthusiasm when the villagers could see that they, rather than the landlord, were effectively benefiting from these projects. On a few occasions it was necessary to protest against cheating or tactless activities of the government officials regarding the voluntary workers.

A representative village committee had been formed, and with it all the problems that arose – bad treatment by some technical supervisors, as well as the fact that one official tried to steal from the funds of the project – were fully discussed before I took steps to remedy the situation at bureaucratic level. The villagers' natural reaction in both these cases was to abandon the whole project and withdraw from participation. Because the problems were solved, the projects could be carried on; and there resulted a greater self-confidence among the villagers and their committee. It remained to be seen, however, whether the authorities would let the representatives defend the village's interests by themselves without my mediation. I had already been warned by higher officials to be careful not to stimulate the peasants too much. There was a danger, they indicated, that the peasants might become *bravo*, bold. In order to keep them 'in their places', these officials suggested the introduction of a charitable programme to replace community self-help efforts.

A test of the extent to which the village leaders could defend their village's best interests came when the govern-

ment officials in charge changed the terms of their promise
to build a school in the village : they reduced the government
contribution and demanded a much greater contribution
from the people than had been originally proposed. When
the village committee was stimulated to try on its own to
arrange for a meeting with the government official in question, the peasant representatives were humiliated and practically thrown out of his office. The peasants were well
aware, so they told me, that this was a proof that basically
nothing had changed for them, and that their habitual distrust was justified. Their resentment increased as a result of
this experience, in which they had participated with considerable cohesion and expectation.

Altogether, from the experience in San Luis, El Salvador,
I had learnt (1) that the peasants' distrust could be overcome,
at least temporarily, by sincerely identifying with their interests and by winning their confidence, and (2) that the
development agency was not really identifying with the
peasants' interests and that the peasants' distrust and their
refusal to collaborate with the agency was only too justified.
A next step would be to find out if peasants are willing to
participate in development activities which are not controlled
by the forces they rightly distrust.

# CHAPTER 3

# A Field Experience in Chile: Distrust Turned into Effective Participation

During a later experience in Chile I learnt by trial and error that peasants can overcome their distrust and get organized, particularly when their efforts are directed against the causes of the distrust. This experiment also showed that distrust and 'resistance to change' could be an asset to effective organization, rather than an obstacle. Distrust, if well understood and appreciated, can be transformed into a dynamic force, uniting the peasants in an effort to bring about a real improvement in their conditions, conflicting with the traditional power structure that attempts to maintain the *status quo*.

The experiment in which this was tried was undertaken while I worked in a community development and agrarian reform project in the Punitaqui valley in the province of Coquimbo in Chile. I worked for one year (1965–6) in the area as a United Nations expert assisting the Chilean government in the setting-up of the project. Initially it encountered serious distrust and resistance from the local population.

In 1964, an agreement between the government of Chile and the United Nations' World Food Programme had been signed to execute a community development project in the Punitaqui valley. The object of the project as stated in this agreement was to develop the agricultural potential of the sixteen communities in the valley with assistance from the World Food Programme (WFP) in the form of surplus food.

The Punitaqui valley belongs to those parts of Coquimbo province where, in the so-called *comunidades agrícolas*, a type of communal land tenure is predominant. The region is also characterized by a very adverse climate. Severe droughts were suffered for so many years running that the government had to take emergency measures, such as food distribution.

The Punitaqui area can be seen as a typical case of 'internal colonialism'. The *comunidades* in that area had, since the second half of the last century, lost most of their fertile valley lands to shrewd large landholders in the region who knew how to secure property rights to large tracts of communal land through legal manipulations. Some of the lawsuits through which the communal peasants (*comuneros*) tried to defend their rights were still going on in 1965. But most of the lawsuits had been lost many years before, through the incapacity of the *comuneros* to pay lawyers to defend their cases in the courts, which traditionally tended to be on the side of the landed elite.

The new situation became legalized in many cases. On the spot it was said that the *comunidad* Punitaqui had lost more than 2,000 hectares of its best lands at the beginning of this century. Although this situation had been 'legalized', a feeling of 'injustice' and resentment about this fact still existed. In some *comunidades* in the Punitaqui valley litigation was still going on. The *comunidad* Potrerillo Alto won back about 1,000 hectares of flat irrigable land through the insistence of its leaders, and another few hundreds of hectares were still in dispute. The *comuneros* of Potrerillo Alto proudly narrated on various occasions how they once, only a few years ago, chased the neighbouring landlord away when he actually started to 'move the fences', in spite of the fact that he threatened them with a pistol. Six other *comunidades* in the valley had such affairs on hand. Only one, however, had won back most of its lands a few decades ago under the leadership of its representative. In 1965 he was a provincial leader of the leftist Federación Campesina e Indígena de Chile, to which most *comunidades* were affiliated.

One result of this whole situation was a strong distrust among the peasants of any outside intervention, particularly since the government had generally been on the side of the large landholding interests (one of the large landholders in the area, still disputing in 1966 with a neighbouring *comunidad* over a large plot of land, was the former vice-president of the country).

In many communities a tradition persisted of common voluntary work. Through such efforts over the years many kilometres of roads and irrigation canals and many schools had been constructed; most schools in the area owe their existence to such common efforts. The tradition was not very strong, however. In the last few years it had been revived somewhat, since the Ministry of Agriculture had stimulated the common cultivation of wheat on parts of the communal land. The harvest was divided according to the days of work which each *comunero* had put up. Because this cultivation was done on a large scale, machinery could be used on credit from the government. Unfortunately, the adverse climate made any wheat cultivation a risky affair, and indebtedness to the government due to bad harvests added to the existing feeling of distrust.

In 1964, when the community development project was initiated in the area, the peasants and their representatives generally declared, in meetings with government officials or among themselves, that they did not want to have anything to do with it. A material incentive of the project was the ration of the World Food Programme which was to be distributed among those *comuneros* who would work voluntarily on community projects. Several communities refused this 'alms' distribution scheme, denouncing it as humiliating, and a device of the government to avoid finding a real solution to the problems of the *comunidades*. Others accepted the food distribution, not as a stimulus to do community work, but as an emergency measure after another drought had killed off a large number of the goats on which they depended for survival.

I tried a new approach in community development, turning the justified resentment and distrust of the *comuneros* into active collaboration in the project. This was not too difficult once the peasants were challenged to give content to the project themselves, so that it would satisfy their basic needs and grievances. A first thing to do was to establish communication with the local peasant leaders and to win their confidence. This was achieved through a straightforward discussion of their most strongly felt grievances. These were not the 'felt needs' for schools, roads and other facilities which were often discussed at meetings, but, as in most rural areas of Latin America, the felt injustices regarding land tenure. However, this obvious grievance initially had to be brought up questioningly in private conversations, in order to be discussed at all. Resentment about these injustices was so deep that the subject was not discussed with foreigners, particularly not with those who came in the context of a government programme. Showing understanding and some measure of appreciation for these grievances was an essential element in establishing the needed communication. I found that the – on the whole well intentioned and dedicated – technicians of the project had never talked frankly with the *comuneros* about their grievances, and were afraid to do so, although they had some kind of understanding of the situation. The technicians were taken along on visits to all the *comunidades*, and they became aware of the basic grievances of the *comuneros* while present at, and participating in, the initial discussions I had with the local leaders or at community assemblies. Soon the technicians participated fully in the open dialogue with the *comuneros* and learnt through this experience that partial technical solutions would be ineffective and that the full collaboration of the *comunidades* could be achieved only by focusing on an overall solution, including the land tenure situation. The *comunidades* would never be able to solve their problems without recovering the fertile lands they had lost in the past which, in modern days, were extensively and inefficiently utilized by a few large landowners. Once the technicians of the project saw this social structural problem clearly, and were willing to discuss the concrete solutions of it with the *comuneros* in their meetings or assemblies, confidence was established and participation of the *comunidades* in the project, including the utilization of the World Food Programme facilities, could be started.

The project technicians were well aware that by taking sides with the *comuneros* against some local vested interests they would create some opposition in the town of Ovalle, but, politicized as they were during their (recent) student years, they took this with good humour and even some pride, after they had overcome their initial hesitation.

The fact that an improved land reform law was under discussion in the National Assembly facilitated a frank exchange of views, since a legally feasible final solution favourable to the peasants was in sight and appeared to be unavoidable.

An additional but equally important factor which helped the peasants to overcome their distrust was the transfer of the management of the World Food Programme facilities at the community level to their elected representatives. After the initial fear and distrust had disappeared, it was not too difficult to convince the project personnel to give considerable active participation and decision-making power to the community representatives. In each community the leaders and the community assembly were given the responsibility for distributing the food ration to those *comuneros* who wanted to participate in the work for the community projects. Moreover, these projects were to be chosen not by the agency but by the community itself in its assembly. The community organizations could thus be considerably strengthened.

Thanks in part to their former syndical or political organization experience the local leaders did very well in the administration of the WFP supplies in the communities, to the surprise of the technicians. These and other arrangements showed the peasants that at least the project technicians working in the area were 'on their side', and were willing to act accordingly.

Altogether, after a few weeks of intensive work in all sixteen communities, local committees had been formed or revived, and were strengthened by being given the responsibility for the monthly emergency distribution of food from the World Food Programme (between August 1965 and January 1966), and the responsibility for the organization of the community works and the proper distribution of food rations, designed as a stimulus for participation in those works. Thus, over the next few months, 7 roads were improved or repaired, 8 schools were built, 5 irrigation canals were constructed or repaired, 2,000 lemon trees were planted, and steps towards the formation of multi-purpose peasant cooperatives were made in several *comunidades*. It should be noted that, although a number of these projects would have been undertaken without the special stimulation from the World Food Programme, the availability of food helped significantly to increase such efforts.

Unfortunately the determination with which the Christian-Democrat government had announced an effective agrarian reform programme, to benefit 100,000 peasants between 1964 and 1970, soon proved to be less strong than it had originally appeared. It took two years simply to get a new land reform law approved in the National Assembly, and then the implementation suffered further delays. Promises regarding the legalization of the boundaries of the *comunidades*, making it possible for them to benefit from the irrigation facilities that were under construction, were executed very slowly, and so were the activities concerning the expropriation of the estates in the area to the benefit of the *comunidades*. Other frustrations were that the materials to be sent by the government agencies to complete the construction of schools and other facilities undertaken by the *comunidades* with local materials arrived after long delays, causing new resentment among the *comuneros*. In all these setbacks the technicians of the project were strongly on the side of the *comuneros* and did all possible to compensate for the mistakes made at the bureaucratic level in Santiago. This helped to maintain to some extent the enthusiasm that had been created but that could not be fully utilized because of the complications at national level.

Shortly before I left the project in 1966 the Federación Campesina e Indígena de Chile (FCI) had organized a regional congress in Ovalle where the participation of the *comunidades* in the project, and the pressure in favour of the needed solution of the land tenure injustices, were strengthened. Although this congress had a lot of political implications, several technicians of the project were willing to participate in the preparatory meetings in the *comunidades* as well as in the congress itself, to explain the purpose of the project and its orientation towards a definitive and radical solution, if the *comuneros* would be willing to push forward. All the former resentments and doubts were brought out again, but now with the wholehearted participation of the *comunidades* in the project, the technicians were able to press for the needed reform measures, which were agreed upon and applauded.

During the next few years the Punitaqui project slowly increased its impact. Several of the estates that were claimed by the *comuneros* at the congress were expropriated, and first steps for the settlement of *comuneros* on those lands were made. But, later, new conflicts arose over the question of whether the *comunidades* would have to pay for the lands assigned to them under the reform programme. They claimed that the lands had formerly been theirs and that they did not need to pay as was usual in the *asentamientos* (land reform settlements) in other areas, where estates were distributed among their former workers. It is not surprising that in 1969 one of the *comunidades*, tired of discussing this issue with the land reform agency (CORA), simply occupied the several hundreds of hectares that it had claimed for many years.

It should be noted that the opposition of the large landowners was on the whole relatively weak, although initially they made a great deal of propaganda for their cause in the local and national press. Well-organized peasant pressure, supported by the project technicians, had resulted, as a side effect, in turning local middle-class public opinion away from the landowners. This, added to the fact that they were to be reimbursed according to the law, forced the landowners to give in. There is little tradition of violence in Chile, and a greater respect for orderly procedure than in most other Latin American countries. For this reason as well, peasant action was less radical than it could have been under other circumstances. It was a long time before the peasants decided upon such a radical act as the seizure of claimed lands. During the Ovalle congress of the FCI, it was clear that the leaders tried to instill moderation and self-control in their followers.

The relative ease with which the peasants of the Punitaqui area were brought to effective action, once they were convinced that this action was part of a broader, overall solution of their main problems and strongly felt needs, shows that there is a considerable potential for peasant mobilization. Of course it cannot be emphasized enough that such mobilization occurs only if the peasants see their effort as a step towards a radical and real solution. This generally means that a conflict situation that has existed for many years, such as the inequality of land tenure, has to be brought into the open and more or less radically solved in favour of the peasants. They also have to be given effective participation in the management of the process of change. Once this opportunity is given to them they will prove able to cope with such responsibilities.

Whether peasant organizations, created to channel a mobilization of the people towards the solution of basic problems, will use radical or moderate means of action seems to depend mainly on the reaction of those who have to give in to their demands.

That the possibility of organized peasant action and even revolt in Latin America is not remote can be seen from several cases where effective movements were created that achieved considerable changes to the benefit of the peasants. In the next chapter the most important peasant movements that have occurred in Latin America will be described.

# CHAPTER 4

# Some Large-Scale Peasant Organizations: Their Origins and Their Effects in Mexico and Bolivia

## 1. THE MEXICAN AGRARIAN MOVEMENT

In this section a description will be given of the peasant guerrillas headed by Emiliano Zapata in the State of Morelos and their struggle for the restitution of lands that had been taken away from them. This movement grew from a village committee defending communal rights into a large-scale organization strong enough to have a considerable impact in the Mexican Revolution of 1910 and to achieve land reform legislation. It had to continue the armed struggle to achieve the implementation of this legislation. After Zapata's death in 1919, the agrarian struggle went on in Mexico until 1934, when President Cárdenas started a large-scale programme of land distribution, supported in this effort by the organized and armed peasants. After his term was over in 1940, the peasant organizations, which had become part of the official government party, were made virtually ineffective because the leadership was taken over or influenced by elements of the traditional or new landowning elite. On some occasions, where independent organizations had a chance to develop, the agrarian struggle flared up again.

1910–1919

The Mexican Revolution, which began in 1910 and in which the armed peasantry played a crucial role, should be seen against the background of the usurpation of communal lands by large haciendas which took place in the second half of the nineteenth century. Many indigenous communities tried in vain to retain or recover the communal lands of which they had been deprived under the legislation which favoured private property. Particularly in the densely populated state of Morelos, the sugar estates expanded at the cost of the communities. The peasants' homes and crops were destroyed to obtain land for sugar cultivation. The peasants affected were forced to work on the estates.

Emiliano Zapata, the son of a small farmer who lost his land in this way, became one of the most outstanding peasant leaders in the area. At the age of thirty he was elected president of the committee of his village, Anenecuilco, which was trying to recover its lost lands. This occurred shortly after Zapata had returned from compulsory military service and work with a *hacendado* in Mexico City, duties which had been imposed upon him as a kind of punishment for his rebellious attitude. During this period Zapata had gained experience and insights which would serve him as a village leader.

Because of his able leadership three other villages with similar problems formed a committee together with Anenecuilco. These villages, led by Zapata, hired a lawyer to defend their rights in the court against the claims of the large haciendas. After years of tedious and fruitless legal struggle, the peasants started to look for other means. Finally they decided to occupy the disputed lands, but – it should be emphasized – only after all legal means had failed. The fear created by the first rumours of national revolt, initiated at that time by Francisco Madero in the north of Mexico, prevented the local authorities from taking action against Zapata and his neighbours in their extra-legal activities.

Madero had started a movement supported by many land-hungry peasant groups against the re-election of Porfirio Díaz to the presidency. The *Plan de San Luis Potosí*, which was the basic declaration of the opposition against Porfirio Díaz, contained a phrase referring to the seizure of the indigenous people's lands: 'Those who acquired lands in so immoral a fashion, or their heirs, will be required to restore them to their original owners, paying them moreover an indemnity for the damage suffered.' After Zapata became acquainted with this revolutionary *Plan de San Luis Potosí*, he and other local leaders organized three guerrilla groups of altogether seventy men to support Madero. After two other leaders had been killed by government troops, Zapata was chosen as commander. Weapons were found in the local haciendas. After a month the group had grown to about a thousand men. Zapata refused to accept money offered as a bribe to calm down his movement. Similar peasant guerrilla groups were operating in other parts of the country. Under pressure from the various rebel armies President Díaz left the country on 26 May 1911.

The land restitution promised by the *Plan de San Luis Potosí*, however, encountered opposition. During his first meeting with the new national leader Francisco Madero, Zapata reminded the President of the land reform promises. In response Zapata was offered an estate which he refused. It seemed that even if Madero himself had been willing to execute the *Plan de San Luis Potosí* with regard to land restitution, for which he had received massive peasant support, the execution would have been difficult, for he was surrounded by many men who belonged to the former government, the military and the landholding families. They boycotted such a programme.

On 20 August 1911 a massive demonstration of 30,000

persons in Mexico City, near the Chapultepec Palace, in favour of Madero and Zapata and against the military and the *hacendados*, requesting the withdrawal of the army from Morelos, did not dissuade the landholding groups from continuing their efforts to crush the peasant movement. Zapata considered his cause betrayed. After escaping from an attempt by the army to capture him in Morelos, he rose again in arms, and soon surprised everybody with the strength of his movement, threatening even the capital.

The way Zapata's troops operated can be compared with modern guerrilla techniques. Whenever a strong army group came close to the guerrillas, they disappeared, either by hiding or by merging with the local population. They had no uniforms and were merely armed peasants, which made it difficult to spot them. At moments when the federal armies did not expect an attack they suddenly appeared and struck. Whenever a town was taken by Zapata's peasant troops, all the records of landownership were purposely destroyed. Practically all the lands of the State of Morelos, fifty-three haciendas, farms and ranches, were given to the peasants. This explains the strong support which the Zapata troops received locally wherever they appeared, and also the strong opposition from the ruling groups in Mexico City. The armed peasants defended the lands which they had obtained when the federal forces came to throw them out.

The rebel groups were not organized in a single army, but in dispersed groups, which were ready to be called upon at any moment and were, in the meantime, cultivating the land they had obtained. By that time Zapata had about 12,000 men, while in the country as a whole there were 150,000 men in the different armies and rebel groups. Zapata's army was probably the largest single military unit, but it was very mobile because of its guerrilla approach. This army sometimes operated as a whole, as during the raid (of 12,000 men) on the rich mines of Hidalgo state. It demonstrated that the government could not even protect the cities within less than a hundred miles of the capital. It sometimes operated in 200 small bands spread over different states. These bands consisted of 30 to 200 men, led by the most energetic *guerrillero*. Some were on foot, others on horseback. Zapata himself often disappeared for days when he went out to inspect the various scattered groups.

Because of Zapata's insistence on the realization of the *Plan de San Luis Potosí*, the *hacendados* of Mexico tried several times to assassinate him and financed a press campaign describing his movement as *bandolerism*, banditry. Zapata and his collaborators recognized as the most effective defence against the accusation of banditry a positive statement clarifying to the world that the peasant movement really stood for social justice. Such a declaration was needed because the government itself was unwilling to fulfil the condition under which the Zapatistas would have given up armed resistance, namely to issue an agrarian reform law as a follow-up of the *Plan de San Luis Potosí*. The new policy statement was drafted in Villa de Ayala. After the idea to launch such a plan developed, the peasant 'generals' (including one Protestant minister), and other villagers present, contributed to the document. The local school teacher, Otilio E. Montaño, wrote this all down in a notebook. Based on suggestions from the peasants, Zapata and Otilio Montaño drafted what became known as the *Plan de Ayala*. The final text was signed in Villa de Ayala on 22 November 1911 and soon after that ratified by all the peasant guerrilla leaders in the mountain camp of Ayoxustla. A local priest made the first typewritten copies.

The *Plan de Ayala* proclaimed that the people should take immediate possession of the lands of which they had been illegally deprived and for which they still could show title. Those who would have difficulty proving their case could receive lands from the expropriation of one third of all the hacienda lands. The lands of those *hacendados* who offered opposition against these measures would be nationalized. Although many lands had been taken by the villages, the first restitution of lands which had officially written evidence based on the *Plan de Ayala* was in Ixcamilpa, State of Puebla, 30 April 1912.

There was a strong reaction from the side of the *hacendados*, who at a meeting of the Mexican Agricultural Chamber decided to form groups of volunteers to combat the peasants. The official armed forces started to deport whole villages in order to suppress the movement.

In 1915, a new government under Carranza tried to weaken and win to its cause the peasant revolutionary forces which practically controlled Mexico City. It published in Veracruz a Decree (6 January 1915) which incorporated the main points of Zapata's programme and which is generally considered to be the formal starting point of the Mexican land reform. This measure, together with the creation of battalions of urban workers which helped the Carranza government to combat the peasant armies, weakened peasant resistance. However, since no real effect was given to the new reform decree, the movement led by Zapata only withdrew from the capital, but retained military control in a large part of the states of Morelos, Guerrero and Puebla. In those areas a land distribution programme was carried out according to the rules of the *Plan de Ayala*, with the help of a group of students of the National School of Agriculture.

Owing partly to the continuous organized pressure of Zapata's troops and to the action of the 'revolutionary generals' in other parts of the country, the ideas of the *Plan de Ayala* were later integrated into the Mexican Constitution (Article 27) of 1917. In spite of this official acceptance, however, effective redistribution of lands took place only in those areas where the peasants were well organized and had some kind of bargaining power, or were armed as in Morelos. After

1917 the persecution of the peasant guerrillas became increasingly intensive. In 1919 Zapata was assassinated by an army officer who had been able to integrate himself into the peasant movement for that purpose. The movement subsequently disintegrated, but more than half of the haciendas in the state of Morelos remained in the possession of the peasants, a situation which was legalized during the following years.

## 1919–1940

After 1919 the opposition of the *hacendados* to agrarian reform took increasingly violent forms. In many areas they formed the so-called 'white guards', bands of armed men who defended the landowners' interests by intimidating or terrorizing the peasants who organized the agrarian committees provided for by the law. The agrarian law stipulated that villagers, in order to obtain land from the haciendas, had to form a so-called 'executive agrarian committee' to send a petition to the competent reform agency. Initially only peasants who were not attached to a hacienda and lived in villages or hamlets, rather than on a hacienda, could petition for land in the area close to their village.

In some of the more densely populated and urbanized states of Mexico, such as Veracruz and Michoacán, the peasants organized themselves against these violent activities. In Veracruz, Ursulo Galván, a peasant's son who had become a labour agitator, organized the peasants into agrarian committees, especially those who tried to petition for land according to law. These committees were brought together in 1923 into the Liga de Comunidades Agrarias del Estado de Veracruz (League of Agrarian Communities of the State of Veracruz). Whereas the governor of Veracruz supported the movement, the military commander of the state was on the side of the landowners. Army units and small bands armed by the landowners terrorized the peasantry in the places where the movement started to grow, and several local leaders were assassinated. When a military coup to overthrow the national government was staged in 1923, with support from the army units in Veracruz, the peasants of the Liga were given arms and organized into a battalion. They effectively helped to defend the government against the generals who started the coup. In the state of Michoacán a similar movement, headed by Primo Tapia, developed in the early twenties.

In 1926 the peasant leagues of Veracruz, Michoacán, and other states that had witnessed similar movements formed the National Peasant League, which was supported by some politicians at national level. In that period many local or regional peasant organizations made their appearance, directed by politicians looking for peasant support as a means of becoming important on the national political scene. Some land was distributed by state governors and many promises were made in an effort to win the peasants' vote or armed support in the political arena. This continued until 1934, when Lázaro Cárdenas became president with the support of several peasant organizations. At the 1934 Convention of the National Revolutionary Party, where Cárdenas was nominated as presidential candidate, peasant representatives, and in particular Graciano Sánchez, managed to introduce changes into the government programme for the next six years, which meant an acceleration of the slow-moving agrarian reform process. These measures included: the speeding-up of land distribution; the creation of an independent Agrarian Department in charge of the reform; participation of peasant representatives in the state agrarian commissions which advised on petitions; and provision for resident workers of haciendas to benefit from agrarian reform.

During the years when most land was distributed – the period 1924–30, and particularly 1934–40 – peasant organizations were able to support their demands effectively. In those periods the government had to rely heavily on the organized and armed peasantry for its defence against several military coups staged by conservative forces opposed to the moderate but firmly reform-oriented regime. The need for armed peasant support to maintain the stability of government was not exaggerated. The *New York Times* reported fifty-three battles between 'agrarianists' and their opponents during the first eighteen months of Cárdenas's government. Several landowners hoped to avoid the distribution of their lands by burning down the villages in which the potential petitioners lived. According to the law, lands of estates within a radius of seven kilometres around a village could be expropriated to the benefit of that village. Several estates tried to take away the legal basis for a petition by making a village disappear or by forcing the inhabitants to move elsewhere.

During Cárdenas's regime, as well as during those of his predecessors, people organizing peasants to make a petition according to the law ran the risk of being assassinated by men hired by the landowners. Even government officials ran this risk. In the first years of Cárdenas's government 2,000 people were reported murdered for such reasons in Veracruz alone. During three critical months in 1936, 500 people were killed in various states.

Responding to a strong need, a Presidential Agreement of 10 July 1935 proposed the formation of peasant leagues, similar to those existing in some parts of the country already. These were to be set up in all the states of the republic and joined into a national peasant federation – Confederación Nacional Campesina (CNC). One of the main purposes of this organization was the unification of all peasants into providing solid support for the government, which was chronically in danger of being overthrown by conservative interests. The CNC membership consisted mainly of the representatives of the beneficiaries of the reform and of the 'executive agrarian committees' which were petitioning for land. The beneficiaries had received land in the form of an *ejido*. The land was the collective property of the village as a whole but could be divided among the villagers for individual cultivation, or be used collectively. Every three years the beneficiaries had to elect a representative body, the *comisariado ejidal*, as a kind of governing board, which also represented the peasants in the CNC and the Ligas at the state level.

Owing to the resistance of the rural elite to the establishment of local organizations, it took three years of organizational work before all the states were represented at a national constituent congress of the CNC in Mexico City in 1938. In the CNC practically all local, regional and national peasant organizations that existed before were brought together, to strengthen themselves, and act as a counterweight to the strongly organized labour movement. Ligas which had been in existence for many years (such as those in the states of Veracruz, Michoacán and Tamaulipas) formed part of the CNC as well as those new Ligas which had been formed as part of the campaign to create the CNC between 1935 and 1938 in the states where there was no such organization before. In some areas the separation of peasant organizations from the workers' organizations of which they had been part, such as in the Comarca Lagunera, brought certain difficulties. However, on the whole a strong and united body emerged.

One of the objectives of the formation of the CNC was to organize the peasants for participation in the national political party, the Party of the Mexican Revolution (PRM), which would support the government. The official party, before, had consisted mainly of government officials who were more or less obliged to join. Cárdenas gave the party a solid mass basis by integrating into it the labour movement, the peasant movement and other groups of the population. This happened in a period when the nation had rallied strongly behind the president because of the crucial issue of the oil expropriation. After serious labour conflicts had occurred which could apparently not be solved, President Cárdenas in 1938 nationalized the foreign oil companies operating in Mexico.

It is probable that political participation, through the CNC, together with the fact that the peasants were armed, created conditions for the vigorous land distribution programme that took place during the years of Cárdenas's presidency. It is also probable that the combination of land distribution and political organization, and the possibility of armed defence by the peasants, laid the foundation in those years for the political stability Mexico has enjoyed since 1940. According to statistics supplied at the end of the Cárdenas regime, a rural militia created by a decree of 1 January 1936 contained 60,000 men in 1940, all with arms and almost half of them with horses. They were organized into about 70 battalions and 75 cavalry regiments, directed by more than 400 chiefs and officers under 9 generals. The function of the rural militia was the organization and control of armed peasant defence. At times the government seemed to have more confidence in the peasant militia than in the regular army. This militia defended the rights of the peasant class, and on several occasions was used to safeguard the national government from severe threats of being overthrown by conservative forces.

It is difficult to say whether the existence of the armed peasant reserve was the reason why a certain measure of peace began to prevail in the country. However, the coincidence between the progress of pacification in the country and official support for the peasant reserve was striking. In particular, the psychological effect on the peasants of legally possessing arms for the defence of their rights should not be underestimated. It helped to overcome their fear of the landowners and their allies.

The speed and determination with which agrarian reform

measures were carried out under Cárdenas, with the whole-hearted participation of representative peasant organizations, created a climate of popular mobilization and enthusiasm. There is evidence that changes occurred in the mentality of the population that could be seen as a kind of collective development 'fever', which was a great asset to extra and voluntary effort.

### After 1940

After 1940 the mobilizing spirit which had inspired the participants and beneficiaries of the new institutions gradually disappeared. Not only had Cárdenas's charismatic leadership ended, but the official political party soon came under the influence of sectors of the middle class that did not see the need to continue the vigorous measures initiated by Cárdenas.

The traditional landholding groups were able to re-establish themselves in new forms, through co-opting government technicians by bribery or other means. And, because of the dishonesty of various government agencies dealing with the *ejidos*, many peasant leaders were unable to resist the temptations of corruption. There is very little evidence that the CNC as an organization has been able to resist this tendency.

One of the main reasons for the limited effectiveness of agrarian reform after 1940 was the fact that the large land-holders were able to conserve or regain considerable strength. Those who were affected by the agrarian reform were generally allowed to choose the best lands for themselves as 'small proprietors'. Their influence in the local power structure was modified, but it was not broken or drastically changed by the appearance of the *comisariado ejidal*. Since government credit facilities were not sufficient to satisfy the needs of the *ejidatarios* (members of *ejidos*), they were dependent on local moneylenders, who were usually directly or indirectly related

to the landholders. At the same time the commercial infrastructure remained in the hands of the rural elite. After
1940 it was not difficult for these groups to gain considerable
influence *within* the political system of Mexico, after their
violent and open resistance *against* it was practically broken
during the Cárdenas years. The acceptance, since 1943, of the
'small proprietors', within the structure of the official party
as part of the 'middle sector', opened a wide field for political
strife in rural areas. The struggle between groups representing opposing class interests was now transferred into the
official party.

In most such cases the CNC did not strongly defend the
peasantry against privileged interests. A great deal depended
on the local leadership. It frequently happened that at the
municipal level (Comité Regional) of the CNC 'small proprietors' or even *hacendados* were able to reach positions of
power within the organization. More frequently, however,
local peasant leaders, attracted by the desire for power and
the symbols of social status, were co-opted by the rural elite.

It could be expected that, since the system which resulted
from the Revolution did not satisfy peasants' needs, new and
more representative organizations would develop to compete
with the post-revolutionary official system. When in 1946
the Partido de la Revolución Mexicana (PRM) was transformed into the Partido Revolucionaria Institucional (PRI),
as a confirmation of the increasing support for and from the
middle sectors, some labour and peasant groups started to
look for other ways of expressing and transmitting their
demands. The Confederación de Trabajadores de México
(CTM), the official Mexican labour union, virtually obliged
its members to vote for the PRI in spite of the presence of
many dissidents in its ranks. It expelled various prominent
leaders when they insisted on the freedom to participate and
vote for the more radically oriented Partido Popular (founded
in 1948). The expelled leaders, Vicente Lombardo Toledano

and Jacinto López, then founded an independent labour and peasant union, Unión General de Campesinos y Obreros de México (UGOCM). Although at its Constituent Congress, 20–22 June 1949, President Alemán was represented by his Minister of the Interior, Ruíz Cortinez, the UGOCM was never legally recognized as a collective bargaining partner by the Labour Ministry. The consequence was that labour unions little by little dissociated themselves from UGOCM. Soon it had only peasant organizations as affiliates.

The UGOCM can thus be considered to be a group which was expelled from the CTM. Its main strongholds among peasants were in areas such as the Comarca Lagunera and Sonora, where peasants had had a direct or indirect relation with the CTM for many years. It was in those areas that the UGOCM found its strength and was able to organize radical activities after the legal approach had failed.

The UGOCM was constantly under pressure from the CNC and other official political institutions. Some of its leaders at local or regional level were assassinated. Others were threatened, and others again were subject to the temptation of lucrative political jobs if they were willing to bring their group into the official organizations. A great deal of factional strife at the village or municipal level occurred as a result of the appearance of the UGOCM. Local leaders and *caciques* tried to avoid or boycott the elections which were to be held periodically in the *ejidos* to renew the leadership. Intimidation and violence were used in this effort. The arbitrariness of local leaders in the country became so alarming that the central government had to intervene. One of the activities during the first three years of the López Mateos government (1958–64) was to renew the membership of 17,000 *comisariados ejidales* and *consejos de vigilancia*.

The need for a revision of the trends which have developed since 1940 has been emphasized even in official statements. It seems to be increasingly urgent, as is shown by the rise of unrest in several areas in Mexico. Although the facts were generally not known beyond a small local circle, some cases of peasant protest and subsequent repression became known through the national press. Among these was the assassination of the peasant leader Rubén Jaramillo and his family in 1962 in the state of Morelos, about 100 miles from Mexico City. A more recent event of this type was the massacre of about twenty-five peasants in Acapulco in 1967. One former president of the PRI observed, in an interview with the *New York Times* of 29 December 1967: 'The public is being "chloroformed" to hide from it the true state of the country. To talk about poverty is "officially forbidden". The peasants have no representative organizations or leaders and the press confines itself to praise the government.'

In spite of the considerable economic progress of Mexico and the large-scale land distribution that have taken place over the last fifty years, there are at present in absolute numbers more landless peasants in Mexico than when the Revolution started.

*Occupation Structure*

|  | 1930 |  | 1960 |  |
|---|---|---|---|---|
| Agricultural workers | 3,626,000 |  | 6,144,000 |  |
| Landless peasants | 2,479,000 | 68% | 3,300,000 | 54% |
| Ejidatarios | 536,000 | 15% | 1,500,000 | 25% |
| Non-*ejidal* owners | 609,000 | 17% | 1,300,000 | 21% |

Source: CIDA – Centro de Investigaciones Agrarias

From 1940 onward government programmes related to agricultural development mainly benefited the growing sector of 'middle' farmers and agricultural entrepreneurs. The existing structure of peasant organizations was utilized to keep the peasants in line with these official policies. It should be noted that the CNC consisted mainly of *ejidatarios*, those who had benefited at least to some extent from land distribution. The three million landless peasants have no representation. Many of the latter category are workers for the 'middle' farmers.

It is clear that the progress of the middle sectors, and on the other hand the marginal participation in development of the majority of the peasantry, creates a situation that is explosive. The Mexican Revolution has gone only half-way. It eliminated the traditional power structure to make way for a more dynamic one, with help from the peasantry. However, it did not give full participation and benefit to the peasants once they were sufficiently under organized control to be manipulated. Forms of 'internal colonialism' are maintained or even extended in many rural areas. Foreign influence on this process has been limited but seems to be increasing.

## 2. THE AGRARIAN MOVEMENT IN BOLIVIA

Many peasant uprisings and agrarian protest movements occurred in Bolivia in the nineteenth and the beginning of the twentieth centuries. All were repressed. The traditional hacienda system maintained itself, and the 'culture of repression' prevailed. Only after the Chaco War in the early thirties had shaken up the country's entire social structure did a modern type of peasant syndicate become effective in some areas – particularly in the Cochabamba valley. The growth of these peasant syndicates, and the ups and downs of the chances for peasant organization and agrarian reform over the years, are the subject of this section.

After the Revolution of 1952, which brought to power a government favourable to peasant demands, the peasant movement grew rapidly. It could only be channelled and controlled by the promotion of a radical land reform programme. After the demand for land was fulfilled, the peasant organization became part of the political structure supporting moderate governments.

## The formation of the peasant syndicates

The Chaco War, fought from 1932 to 1935 between Bolivia and Paraguay over a large border area, disturbed the *status quo* of semi-feudal and caste-like social relationships. Bolivia's defeat made many people aware of the weakness of the traditional social system. The participation of many Indians among the 100,000 Bolivians who served in the army and supply lines, and the propaganda directed towards the Indian soldiers to stimulate them, created a new consciousness among the indigenous people of their relations with the 'whites', who often depended on them in critical situations.

In 1936 the first rural syndicate was formed in Ucureña, close to Cochabamba, in the latifundio Santa Clara. A school was also started. Parts of the latifundio, belonging to a monastery, had been leased to a local landholder who exploited the peasants tied to the land in an abusive way. This abuse caused discontent, particularly after the combatants of the Chaco War had returned. One of the additional reasons why a union could be formed more easily in the Santa Clara estate (and also at more or less the same time in the Vacas estate in the province of Arani) than elsewhere was the fact that there was not one traditional landlord to whom the peasants were tied, but rather a group of owners. There was a less personal relationship between the peasants and the *patrón*.

Another factor was that even before the Chaco War the monastery had sold a few plots to small peasants called *piqueros*, who through the purchase of this land became independent. This sale was frowned on by the large landowners of the area.

The local peasants, in order to free themselves from the feudal obligations of service, got together under the leadership of the Delgadillo brothers to form a syndicate to lease the land themselves from the Santa Clara monastery. They received help from a school teacher, from students of Cochabamba and from Eduardo Arze Loureiro, the son of a landowner, who was open to new ideas. He was helpful in the tedious legal procedures necessary to obtain the lease for the union. However, the new arrangement worked for only a few years. In 1939 a small group of landowners got together to destroy the nascent syndicate and remove the threat to the customary pattern of landlord rule. With help from the government, they prevailed upon the Santa Clara convent to sell the land to them so that they could abandon the legal arrangement made by the union and its helpers. They cleared the land and destroyed the houses of the peasants (who had been living there for generations) under the pretext of 'rationalizing' the cultivation. Those peasants who did not want to work again for the hacienda were driven from the land. Twelve peasant leaders were confined to an isolated area of the country in 1940. This attack brought more awareness to the peasants that they were repressed as a group.

In the difficult period during and after 1940, the syndicate became increasingly dependent on the leadership of the local school director, Juan Guerra, who became a member of the Party of the Revolutionary Left (PIR). With assistance from from various intellectuals of the town of Cochabamba, Guerra helped the peasants to purchase some parts of the estate, although for a price higher than the landowners would have paid. About 200 peasants thus became the owners of one-hectare plots and gained independence from the *patrón*. Guerra also helped peasants of surrounding estates to channel to the authorities their complaints about landlords' abuses. The union's influence spread and, in turn, it helped in the founding of various smaller schools, related to the *nucleo escolar* (central school) in Ucureña.

The syndicate regained its strength and developed further under the able leadership of José Rojas, a native of Ucureña who had been driven from the hacienda on which his father had been a *colono*. Rojas escaped to Argentina but returned secretly to Ucureña later in the 1940s.

Around 1940 various new political parties had been formed in exile. Among these was the Partido de Izquierda Revolucionario (PIR, Party of the Revolutionary Left), founded in 1940 under the leadership of the sociologist José Antonio Arze (who called himself an independent Marxist), while the Partido Obrero Revolucionario (POR, Revolutionary Workers Party), of Trotskyite orientation, became influential in those years through Juan Lechín, the leader of the Miners' Federation. The Movimiento Nacionalista Revolucionario (MNR), founded by a group of intellectuals headed by Víctor Paz Estenssoro, was a mixture of liberal intellectuals and young army officers who were dissatisfied with the mishandling of the Chaco War. It was later joined by tin miners and groups of the much-divided PIR. When the government of Enrique Peñaranda, after having declared war on the Axis powers, was overthrown in 1943, Major Gualberto Villarroel became president. He took several leaders of the MNR into his government, while repressing both the traditional and the Marxist parties.

During the government of Villarroel, which came to power on 20 December 1943 and in which Paz Estenssoro participated, several events contributed to the increasing awareness and organization of the peasantry. In August 1944, Paz Estenssoro and Walter Guevara Arce presented to the National Convention a proposal for a moderate agrarian programme. Opposition from the majority in the Convention controlled by the powerful organization of large landholders, the Sociedad Rural Boliviana, was strong enough to block

acceptance of the proposal. But the Movimiento Nacionalista
Revolucionario, led by Paz and Guevara, which defended the
proposal awakened the peasantry to the fact that they had
allies. Land reform became a cause to struggle for with more
effective means than spontaneous uprisings.

Another event which seemed to confirm this tendency was
the organization in the beginning of 1945 of the first Indian
Congress, organized by the Indian leader Luis Ramos
Quevedo. The congress started on 10 May 1945 with approximately 1,000 delegates from all ninety-eight provinces. The
main points of the agenda were: abolition of the unpaid
personal services which peasants had to render to landlords;
education; regulation of agricultural labour conditions and
agrarian policy. No radical measures were proposed by the
peasant delegates, but demands made were directed against
the most abusive forms of servitude and lack of educational
facilities. As a result of the Congress, government decrees
were issued which abolished unpaid personal services and
obliged the landlords to establish schools on the large
haciendas. Land reform as such was not dealt with.

The opposition of the conservative forces to the new
decrees and other proposed measures became increasingly
strong. Little or no implementation was given to the decrees
which were promulgated by the government as a result of
the Indian Congress, particularly Decree 319 which abolished
*pongueaje* and other forms of unpaid services to the landlords.

In the period of the Indian Congress, many of the spontaneous peasant movements and uprisings against the landholders, and also the struggles between indigenous communities over boundaries, calmed down or even disappeared.
The negative reaction of the landlords after the Indian Congress provoked sit-down strikes (*huelga de brazos caídos*),
covering large areas in Tarija, Oruro and Potosí. These strikes
implied a refusal to render unpaid personal services, *de facto*

fulfilling the decrees issued in May 1945. Indian peasant organizers, especially those who had experience as miners, travelled around in many areas to awaken the peasantry. Political organizers of the MNR also participated in this campaign. The press spread fear of the indigenous movements among the urban middle class, exaggerating them in order to discredit the government which tolerated them. This counter-action was largely responsible for the overthrow of the re-formist government on 21 July 1946 and the assassination of President Villarroel. All the measures decreed during the previous years were cancelled, and the traditional situation was restored in the rural areas.

The peasant protest movements which occurred after 1946, as a reaction to the change of government, were met by armed force. Many peasant leaders, particularly those who had participated in the Indian Congress, were jailed. Revolts, protesting against these new developments, started at the end of 1946. In Ayopaya, Cochabamba, several thousand peasants invaded large landholdings and assassinated a landlord who forcibly tried to reintroduce the feudal obligations. In the Los Andes province of La Paz, similar protest actions took place after the landowners had refused to negotiate the peti-tions. From then on, most of the peasant movements took on a violent character, thus shedding their former stance of non-violence. Landlords' houses on estates and even some pro-vincial capitals were threatened or effectively attacked. Miners had an important leadership function in the move-ments.

The objectives of the movements at this stage went beyond mere changes in working conditions. Their demands included radical change in the political and social structure of the country. The intransigence of the landowners had apparently provoked a strong awakening of the peasants. Workers from La Paz who were affiliated to the Federación Obrera Local, related to the MNR, helped to organize the peasant protest movements on the Altiplano. Several labour leaders active in this field were jailed.

The movements in various parts of the country were repressed by large-scale military intervention. A special rural police corps was created. About 250 peasant leaders were sent to a 'penal colony' in Ichilo, created in the jungle for this purpose. During the years of turmoil between 1946 and 1952 the MNR remained illegal and attempted several times to overthrow the regime. Then, in the presidential elections of 1951, Paz Estenssoro won forty-five per cent of the vote. The military junta which took over in order to prevent the MNR from coming to power through legal means lasted only eleven months, until General Antonio Seleme, chief of the Carabineros, or national military police, went over to the MNR. In April 1952, a violent revolution broke out with street fighting between the army on one side and on the other the Carabineros and armed miners, trade unionists, and other wage earners of the city, as well as small shopkeepers and members of the middle class.

About two weeks later Paz Estenssoro returned from Argentina and became president. Some estimates suggest that 3,000 people were killed in the turmoil. In some of the areas close to La Paz, such as Achacalla and Patamanta, peasants had joined the struggle of the other groups which brought about the revolution.

Quite soon after the new government had taken power, amnesty was given to the peasant leaders who were in concentration camps because they had participated in protest movements which occurred in different places between 1946 and 1952.

In the meantime the MNR tried to get control of the growing peasant syndicate movement in the Cochabamba area by trying to replace José Rojas as head of the syndicate by a moderate leader. However, at a meeting in Cliza, the provincial capital, Rojas won and became the undisputed leader of the Sindicato Campesino de Ucureña del Valle. The Ucureña syndicate sent out many peasant leaders and MNR students from Cochabamba to the surrounding areas to create new syndicates and to carry the news of the revolution of April 1952.

## From 1952 onwards

Immediately after the coming to power of the MNR on 12 April 1952, a Ministry of Peasant Affairs was created. It is curious that the formation of peasant unions was not officially included among the objectives of this Ministry, and neither was agrarian reform. However, these fields became its main concern after considerable peasant pressure in favour of radical reform. This pressure was a reaction to the intransigence shown by the landlords after April 1952, particularly in the Cochabamba area.

When the Ucureña syndicate requested that holdings be returned to those peasants who had been driven from their land, the landowner refused. A general uprising was called for. The peasants of three provinces threatened to invade the town of Cliza and burn the houses of the local landowners. The sub-prefect of Cliza succeeded in pacifying the peasants, but once they were aware of their strength acts of violence became more frequent. An incident which gave the movement a strong impetus occurred in Chilicchi, close to Cliza and Ucureña. A landowner locked up a worker because he had not brought his tools with him to work. The peasants organized a machete-waving demonstration to free their colleague. They became so threatening that the landowner fled, leaving everything behind. Such demonstrations occurred more and more frequently, the peasants taking over the lands immediately and transforming the hacienda houses into syndicate centres, schools or hospitals. The leaders were not able to restrain their followers.

After a few months 1,200 syndicates were active in the department of Cochabamba, with 200,000 members. This movement, and the violence which accompanied it in some instances, should be seen as a reaction to the efforts of the landed elite, particularly in Cochabamba, to organize an armed counter-revolution. The violence which occurred was, according to the reports of the ministry, due to the anxiety of the peasants to defend the new regime, which promised them agrarian reform and the abolition of servitude. There was no evidence of mob acts of vengeance for past abuses and injustices suffered, although in some of the scattered cases of looting revenge may have played a role. Given the desire of the peasants to undo ages of repression, it was difficult for the peasant leaders to check the movement and channel its energy in an orderly way.

The activities of the peasant syndicates, occupying haciendas and demonstrating in the towns, took place mainly during the first half of 1953. This movement strongly alarmed the landowners, many of whom fled to the cities leaving house and land to the peasants, who armed themselves with the weapons they found in the haciendas.

The new government saw that only an overall land reform eliminating the hacienda system could channel and control the rising tide of peasant unrest. A commission was nominated which drafted in a few months a radical land reform law. In connection with the carrying-out of this reform, and in order to gain the support of the peasantry as a whole, the new Ministry of Peasant Affairs started a campaign to organize the peasants all over the country into syndicates. An agreement between the government and the newly created Central Obrera Boliviana, in which Juan Lechín had great influence, arranged for many of the mine workers who had worked in unionization (most of whom were former peasants and spoke the indigenous language) to travel all over the country to help create the peasant syndicates. They prepared meetings, and peasants of several communities and haciendas were called together by *pututu* (the traditional horn). Then a commission of the Ministry of Peasant Affairs came to institutionalize the new syndicates. Participants in this campaign testify to the enthusiasm with which the peasants, traditionally accustomed to gatherings of this kind dealing with community affairs, responded. In several areas an indulgence in legalistic procedures was encountered. The peasant leaders were not content until their syndicates were recognized, with all the signatures of local authorities and the Ministry of Peasant Affairs obtained.

The whole campaign culminated in the ceremony of the promulgation of the land reform decree (Decreto Supremo No. 3464) on 2 August 1953 in Ucureña, where, according to some sources, 200,000 peasants were present, one third of them with their weapons. Peasants from all over the country could see there with their own eyes how their colleagues in the Ucureña area and around had already effective control over the lands which they had seized from the latifundia.

Since the government needed peasant support against conservative forces attempting to overthrow it, the weapons of the dissolved army were given to newly formed peasant units. Also, the miners obtained an important share of the arms. The experience gained by peasants and miners during the Chaco War made the formation of these new defence units relatively easy. One objective was to impress the citizenry of the larger towns with the growing strength of the peasantry, as happened for example during a march of peasants through La Paz on 9 April 1953.

Already, before the official promulgation of the agrarian reform decree, latifundia had been taken over by the peasants in some areas, such as the Cochabamba valley. Once the decree was issued, this procedure was legalized. An accelerated taking-over of latifundia was promoted by the government all over the country. Latifundia were abolished and divided among those who had worked on them. The parts already possessed by the peasants, as *sayañas* in exchange for free labour on the owner's land, would be theirs immediately. Of the rest of the estate, each would get a share. A parcel for collective use and for the school would be set apart. The unpaid labour obligations were abolished.

While latifundia were no longer permitted, small and medium private properties and well-exploited agricultural enterprises would be respected by the law, and in most cases were in fact respected by the peasants. In estates where the relationship between landlord and the peasant had been relatively cordial, arrangements could often be made to guarantee a continuation of the production of the estate for mutual benefit. Where the landlords had been abusive and tension existed between the two parties, the landlord and his family generally left the estate for fear of possible reprisals.

The law was put into effect with help from the syndicates that had been or were being formed in all parts of the country. In those areas where peasant syndicates did not yet exist when the land reform decree was promulgated, they were organized from above. On 15 July 1953 the Confederación Nacional de Trabajadores Campesinos de Bolivia (CNTCB) was founded with the help of the Ministry of Peasant Affairs. The top leaders helped to form federations in departments where they did not yet exist. After the reform decree had been promulgated, it was explained to the peasants at mass meetings how they should go about the land reform, and occupy immediately the latifundia in expectation of the legal transfer of title, which would follow later. People who participated in this campaign testified to the enthusiastic response of the peasantry and their ability to take their fate into their own hands. Since most landlords were afraid of reprisals and had fled to the city, the syndicates had to fill the vacuum that resulted in the local power structure. They assumed responsibility for running that part of the estate that was formerly managed by the landlord or his administrator. The whole process was accomplished in less than a year.

The president of the National Agrarian Reform Council estimated in 1955 that 324,355 peasants had automatically benefited with 973,065 hectares of land that they had worked formerly in exchange for unpaid labour. An automatic consequence of the law was that a number of the leaders of the MNR Party lost their own or their family's land, among them President Paz Estenssoro and the Minister of Peasant Affairs, Ñuflo Chavez. This made a big impression on many people.

The rate at which the programme was applied prevented opposition from becoming violent or gaining strength. In the small urban centres the peasant marches, often armed, convinced the merchants and other townsmen of the fact that power had effectively been taken over by the peasantry and its leaders.

The consolidation of a new political system after the 1952 Revolution eliminated the traditional domination of the rural areas by the landlords, and a greater freedom of the peasantry resulted. Expressions of this freedom, in addition to the absence of landlord domination, were the disappearance of the designation 'Indian', which was replaced by the term *campesino* (peasant), and the extension of the right to vote to illiterate people.

From 1952 the peasant organizations were closely related with the government as well as with the Movimiento Nacionalista Revolucionario, the government party for many years. The exact nature of this relationship is unclear, particularly since 1964. The CNTCB has supported the government rather than the party in power, as long as the government did not antagonize the peasants' interests. Since practically all land available for the land reform programme has been distributed and what remains to be done in over half of the cases is the granting of a legal title, peasants are more or less satisfied and will remain so as long as the new structure created in 1952 is not changed.

One of the main problems which keeps the peasants alert and prepared to defend their interests is the fact that, although by mid-1954 practically all latifundio land had been taken over by the beneficiaries of the agrarian reform, the process of the distribution of property titles to these lands has been slow. By 1966 approximately 170,000 peasant families, only half of those who received land, had benefited from the title distribution; the cases of the other half were still pending.

This insecurity of title possession was one argument used by parliamentary peasant representatives to defend the right of peasants to carry arms in Bolivia. As long as there are some plots possessed by the peasants according to the agrarian reform law which have not been duly legalized as their property, the former landlords may try to reverse the process of land distribution. In personal talks some of these representatives confessed in 1966 that the lack of a stable government, and subsequent doubts about its intentions (possibilities of an increase in 'illegitimacy'), was reason enough for the peasants to keep their arms as a guarantee that their interests would not be impinged upon.

This made it possible, on some occasions, for local peasant unions to overrule top-level leaders who had approved the introduction of a land tax for the small peasant owners in 1968. Opposition at the base against this measure was so strong that, in Bélen and in Achacachi, the top leaders of the CNTCB and President Barrientos himself had to flee to avoid violence from a peasant assembly which the president had addressed to explain the need for the tax.

Compared with the situation before 1952, the peasants in

Bolivia had on the whole benefited much more from land reform than those in Mexico. The great majority of the Bolivian peasants were transformed from semi-feudal serfs into small proprietors. The improvement in living conditions, particularly the nourishment of the peasantry, was so obvious that the average size of the army recruits increased notably in the years after the land distribution. The peasants simply ate a good deal more, which was also one of the reasons for the temporary decrease in marketed agricultural produce in the first post-reform years. In spite of radical changes in the rural areas, the fundamental problems of the Bolivian economy remained unsolved. These were, however, not so much in the agricultural sector but rather in mining, on which the country depends heavily. Although the major tin mines were nationalized after 1952, the dependence on foreign controlled markets remained the same or increased, which prevented the country from making a complete change in its social structure. While the mine workers' unions continued to struggle for more radical and fundamental changes in Bolivian society, the peasant unions, after they had benefited from the land reform, were on some occasions utilized to appease or even combat the miners. This happened particularly after 1964. Once the peasants receive land through agrarian reform, they seem to lose interest in promoting further revolutionary change in society as a whole.

## 3. MEXICO AND BOLIVIA COMPARED

In both Mexico and Bolivia, peasant organizations initially grew and became strong in a spontaneous way, uncontrolled by the government. Only later were they institutionalized as part of the national/political system, after this system had undergone considerable and drastic change. In both countries the peasant organizations had a certain influence on the creation of the new political structure which arose after the revolutionary changes. The peasants initially won significant benefits, mainly land distribution. As a result they were so indebted to the new system that they supported it, in spite of the fact that the flow of further benefits was very small. They continued to live on the margin of society, although somewhat better off than in the pre-revolutionary situation.

The role of peasant organizations in post-reform Mexico and Bolivia has been limited. In neither country did the peasants gain an influence in national policy-making which corresponded to their numerical force.

Peasants and their organizations have been helpful in bringing about a change in the traditional social structure, opening up possibilities for a more dynamic development of the country as a whole. However, after the transfer of most or part of the political power from the traditional elite into the hands of more dynamic groups (generally middle-sector), the peasantry was neutralized as a political force. The potential for peasant mobilization after the reform has, on the whole, not been realized except in a few periods, such as in Mexico under the Cárdenas regime. Rather, emphasis has been placed on consolidation and the institutionalization of the peasantry's role as a political supporter of the new elites.

From the outset the Mexican and Bolivian peasant organizations were strongly related to the agrarian reform process and were recognized, or institutionalized, by the agrarian reform laws. Membership became almost obligatory for those peasants who did not participate in the initial spontaneously growing organizations.

The Bolivian agrarian reform was not only different from the Mexican but in many respects quite opposite to it in its approach. In Mexico only in critical stages, such as the initiation of the agrarian revolution in the period between 1910 and 1919, and in some particular instances later, did

*de facto* distribution of land precede the completion of the
legal procedure.

On the whole, in Mexico, the process of *de facto* land distribution was even slower than the legal assignment of *ejido*
lands, which could take several years. As a result, many
peasant villages lived for years in insecurity and tension.
Opposition of vested interests to land distribution generally
did not stop until the land was effectively given over to the
peasants in an official ceremony.

In Bolivia the actual reform process was started before
the law was passed. Once an appropriate law existed, the
peasants could effectively and legitimately take possession of
the land before the legal transfer of the title from the landowner to the reform beneficiaries.

Another contrast between the approach in the two
countries is that in Mexico the main stress of the agrarian
reform initially was to return the lands to the *comunidades*
or to those peasants who had lost it in earlier years. Only
from 1934 onwards were the *peones acasillados*, the peons
who lived on and were tied to the haciendas, affected by possible land distribution. This was almost twenty years after
the first agrarian law was passed. On several occasions these
*acasillados* had been used by the landlords to combat groups
of peasants who claimed land lawfully. The agrarian reform
decree of 1953 in Bolivia also gave due satisfaction to the
needs of the *comunidades* to recover their original lands, but
it supported particularly the peasants who lived on the
haciendas, were tied to the land and had been obliged to
serve the landlord. The break with the traditional system
was much more drastic and immediate than in Mexico. This
probably explains why the Bolivian reform did not provoke
the violent struggle that swept Mexico for years. Landlord
opposition in Bolivia was eliminated in a relatively short
time by the organized and armed peasantry.

The difference between Mexico and Bolivia regarding land

reform may have been due partly to the fact that in Mexico there was initially no united and organized group or party with a more or less specific purpose or ideology behind the revolution. The Mexican national party was formed a decade after the severest revolutionary turmoil was over. In Bolivia the revolutionary party, the MNR, had been struggling and winning support from urban labour and some peasant groups long before the Revolution of 1952. It seems, however, that the radical peasant action in Cochabamba pushed the MNR beyond its original intentions regarding land reform.

While in Mexico it took fifty years of ups and downs in agrarian reform to come to a stage where most of the land concerned had been distributed, in Bolivia the latifundia system was *de facto* abolished in 1952–3 in a sweeping campaign that probably lasted altogether less than a year.

# CHAPTER 5

# Other Peasant Organizations and Movements

The Mexican and Bolivian agrarian movements show particularly well what is possible in the formation of effective peasant organizations. Both movements had their impetus from below. Only after they gained strength on their own account did the government support and help extend the organizations. Both movements were quite successful in achieving large-scale land distribution. They were neutralized as part of a new 'establishment' only after their original demands were largely fulfilled. In order to give perspective to the generalized conclusions to be drawn from these more or less successful experiences, it will be useful to consider the few other, less successful or less authentic peasant movements that have occurred in Latin America.

One of these is the peasant federation that has been functioning in Venezuela with ups and downs from about 1945 until the present. This federation was not a peasant movement that grew from below as a reaction to the 'culture of repression', but was organized from the outset by urban politicians. During and after ten years of repression, it became quite militant and achieved considerable gains, such as land distribution, for many peasant groups.

In the Peruvian highlands, particularly in the valley of La Convención, a movement grew that could have followed the Bolivian pattern if the Peruvian government had not halted it by a localized land distribution, or promises to that effect, and large-scale army intervention. The movement did not reach national proportions, but the way it grew from below and particularly the methods of struggle it applied, such as the occupation of disputed lands, are important for the study of the possibilities of peasant organization in Latin America.

Another important movement, almost completely destroyed in 1964, was the formation of Peasant Leagues in north-east Brazil. This movement grew from below, along more or less similar lines to other movements, but before it became a well-structured organization it was crushed by the opposition of conservative forces. The same happened to a lesser extent with competing movements that were created by the church in the same region to neutralize the influence of the Leagues. To study how a peasant movement can grow in a region where the traditional patronage system weighs heavily on the peasants, the Leagues of north-east Brazil are a particularly useful example.

In some countries, especially in Colombia and Guatemala, peasants have been in movement in more or less unstructured ways, resulting in considerable violence. These cases show how violent reaction on the part of the peasants is not so much an inherent characteristic of their movements, but results from the fact that the landed elite makes the orderly development of representative peasant-interest groups impossible, either by provoking struggles between groups or through repression. In Colombia there was a great deal of violence after a populist leader who could well have channelled peasant discontent in an organized fashion was assassinated in 1948. In Guatemala violence was used to undo the effects of the agrarian reform and peasant organization drive that was introduced by a populist government in the early fifties.

Particularly when looking at the 'revolutionary potential' of peasants (as will be done in Chapter 7) it is important to consider the reactions of the peasants in Colombia and

Guatemala, although for the time being no organized or structured movements exist in those countries.

## 1. VENEZUELA: THE PEASANT FEDERATION

Contrary to what happened in Mexico and Bolivia, peasant organization in Venezuela was initiated and stimulated from above as part of the national political system. The whole peasant movement was organized as an electoral clientele for the reformist Acción Democrática (AD) party, which used its political influence to procure certain benefits in order to win adherence for the Federación Campesina de Venezuela (FCV) it created.

During the government of Juan Vicente Gómez (1909–35) there was already a good deal of unrest in Venezuelan rural areas. This was largely due to the frustration felt by the squatters on formerly virgin land (*conqueros*) who were forced into peonage at a time when large landholders were receiving property titles to thousands of hectares of such land. In the 1930s there was evidence of land invasions by peasants, and the number of conflicts between *conqueros* and sharecroppers, tenants and landowners over tenure conditions grew rapidly. A movement started among wage labourers towards a militant unionization, and in several places scattered eruptions of violence were noted. Some were violently repressed; but an unintended consequence of the government's policy of repression was an increased potential for militant organized action by the peasants.

The group of political leaders around Rómulo Betancourt, who had returned to Venezuela after Gómez's death, saw in this potential a means of winning mass support for the political party which they were organizing, and which later became Acción Democrática. The formation of a national peasant organization was an important aspect of their campaign. Betancourt himself, according to many informants, played an active role in the establishment of peasant syndicates on a national scale. A liberal labour law, passed in 1936 by Gómez's successor General Elías López Contreras, made rural unionization legally possible, although the law had such strict operating requirements that at times more local unions lost their legal personality than were recognized. The increase of officially existing unions was thus rather slow. The number rose between 1936 and 1945 from 3 unions (with 482 members) to 77 (with 6,279 members).

Many difficulties were encountered in those years by the initiators and charismatic leaders, such as Ramón Quijada. Union activities were often considered illegal and politically subversive by local authorities and national guard commanders. They were often repressed. The men who led the movement during this period took great risks. As a result of their efforts it could be claimed that in 1945 there existed 500 groups, with about 100,000 members.

This strength was built up by about 200 professional organizers, who were sent out to recruit local leaders able to mobilize the peasants effectively. Initially this was done mainly in the areas of greatest population pressure and concentrated holdings – the states of Aragua and Carabobo – where great numbers of peasants came into conflict with the large landowners over tenancy or sharecropping conditions. It was in areas where the peasants were relatively advanced that pressures were most strongly manifested. The tenants and sharecroppers appeared to respond more vigorously to agitation than the squatters in more remote areas or the wage labourers on commercial farms. In areas ready for organization, local leaders were approached with offers to help organize the peasants into effective peasant unions, related to the nationwide peasant and labour movement that was part of Rómulo Betancourt's reform-oriented political movement. When in October 1945 Betancourt became president after a *coup d'état* organized jointly by his party and a group of dissident army officers, a strong impetus was given to the labour and peasant movement that mainly benefited the unions of AD orientation. The mobilization of the voters behind the Acción Democrática proved to be successful: in 1946 this party received 80 per cent of the popular vote. Under the AD government, between 1945 and 1948 the number of legally recognized peasant unions increased from 77 to 515, with 43,302 members – still less than ten per cent of all peasants in the country. In 1947 at the national level the Federación Campesina de Venezuela was formed, with Ramón Quijada as its first president.

In the years between 1945 and 1948 a number of measures helped to strengthen the peasant union movement significantly. Through various decrees, arrangements were made to lease under favourable conditions to peasant union members lands belonging to the government (such as those formerly owned by Gómez) and also privately-owned land which was not actively farmed. Thus, by the end of 1948, an estimated 125,000 hectares of land had been leased to approximately 73,000 union members. In addition, through the Instituto Tecnico de Inmigración y Colonización (ITIC), large sums were made available to farm these leased lands. The credits were distributed locally by committees consisting of a representative from ITIC, a credit specialist, and an official from the peasant syndicate, who had the responsibility of verifying the performance of the applicant in the tasks assigned in the technical farm plan drawn up by ITIC.

These arrangements gave great power, status and prestige to the local peasant union leaders. Recruited initially as social and opinion leaders in their rural communities, these people, by virtue of their connections with the government, had been granted powerful instrumental attributes: as leaders in forming the syndicates they could choose the peasants whom they desired as members; they also could petition the ITIC for land grants for members to farm, and were in a position to influence the granting and control of the accompanying farm credits.

In October 1948 an Agrarian Reform Law was passed which could have had a significant effect if it had not been for the overthrow of the Acción Democrática government by Lt-Col. Charles Delgado and Lt-Col. Marcos Pérez Jiménez, both of whom had helped to bring Betancourt to power, but who wanted to impose restraint on the Acción Democrática government. In the years following, the peasant and labour movements were again severely repressed. The executive committees of all the 515 peasant syndicates were dissolved. The effects of the initial steps of agrarian reform made in the previous years were mostly undone. A great part of the government land, which was being leased under favourable terms to members of the unions, was recaptured by the members of the Gómez family. Private lands for which reasonable leasing conditions had been obtained could again be used by the owners as they saw fit. Eviction of peasants from such lands, occasionally accompanied by violence, was not rare.

The experience of repression, however, indirectly helped to strengthen the peasant movement. Immediately after the fall of the Pérez Jiménez regime in 1958, the peasant unions of the FCV, which had been organized clandestinely for about ten years, came into the open apparently stronger than ever. In the few areas where land had been taken from the peasants between 1948 and 1958, peasant unions simply recovered the lands. Competition existed between various political groups for peasant support, and this resulted in the more radical groups, which most forcefully represented the peasants' demand for land, setting the tone. Because of fear of competition from Christian-Democrat and Communist forces, Acción Democrática peasant groups began to take over lands claimed by their members.

Rómulo Betancourt, who became president again in 1958,

condemned the invasions, branding them as violence. He expressed the hope that the leaders of the Federación Campesina de Venezuela, at that time organizing a national peasant congress, would prove a moderating influence. On 2 June 1959 the First Venezuelan Peasant Congress, organized by the FCV, accepted a strongly worded resolution demanding land reform legislation. It also decided on the active mobilization of the peasants all over the country to prepare the petitions for land. The pressure was so strong that to get ahead of the invasions, the land reform agency (Instituto Agrario Nacional), gave land to 24,000 families in its first year. It had planned to settle only 10,000. Only provisional titles were given out in that period and the distribution of the lands of each estate among the peasants was initially left to the union or committee which had presented the petition, or had organized the occupation of their estate.

While most invasions took place in 1958 and 1959 immediately after Pérez Jiménez's fall, they continued after the promulgation of the land reform law in 1960. The government had to find a way of dealing with this. While in very few cases invasions were repressed or halted by public force, elsewhere they were channelled or avoided by finding a solution to the problem before the peasants had taken radical action. Some cases are known, such as the pilot project La Julia-Jobo Dulce, where the public forces were present when the invasion took place and watched that everything occurred in an orderly way. Opposition by the landowners was generally limited. The change in the political climate in the country after the fall of the Pérez Jiménez regime and the strong public opinion in favour of radical changes in the rural areas, in addition to the sweeping action undertaken by the FCV peasant unions, made it clear to the landlords that opposition would be useless and that immediate sale of lands to the Instituto Agrario Nacional, rather than waiting for expropriation, would be convenient.

According to studies made in 1966, of the 761 landholdings acquired by IAN for land distribution, about one third, 256, had been invaded, mainly in the years 1959–61. The invasions which took place in those years covered approximately 60 to 70 per cent of the landholdings acquired for reform in those years. They occurred mainly in the areas where urban influences were strongest, such as those states where more than two thirds of the population lived in cities. Thus, 203 land invasions, almost 80 per cent of the total of 265, took place in the states of Aragua, Carabobo, Yaracuy, Trujillo and Zulia, where peasant unions were most strongly organized. Half of the invasions took place before the law was passed and were influential in accelerating its acceptance. In several instances, the frequency of which is difficult to estimate, the invasions were favoured by the landholders because the sale of their land to the Instituto Agrario Nacional extracted good prices, particularly in areas close to the cities.

By 1961, leadership problems emerged within the FCV concerning what policy to follow. One of the issues was the speed of agrarian reform. Some leaders wanted to agitate for a more rapid and drastic agrarian reform programme. But soon the more radical leadership elements were purged, particularly at the local level. Urban labour leaders were brought in to replace them. Ramón Quijada, the national president of the FCV, was replaced by Armando González, who followed a less radical line with regard to land reform.

The change was related to lack of money to remunerate the landowners according to the legally established high rates. In 1962 it was decreed that no more invaded lands would be used for land reform purposes, which practically brought the invasions to an end. After the purge of the leadership of the FCV at all levels, the moderation in the demand for land distribution was transmitted through the FCV to the peasantry, apparently with success. The most active and organized areas had been satisfied during the first years of the reform and the de-emphasizing of the importance of accelerated land distribution did not encounter much opposition after the more radical leaders had been replaced. The FCV then became increasingly an instrument through which benefits such as credits, schools, roads and other facilities could be channelled to the peasant clientele, in exchange for votes to the government parties.

## 2. THE PERUVIAN HIGHLANDS: THE PEASANT MOVEMENT IN LA CONVENCIÓN AND OTHER AREAS

In many areas of Peru there persists to this day the system of including personal services as part of the peasants' obligations to the landlord. Thus in the valley of La Convención and Lares, department of Cuzco, there were 174 haciendas with much idle land which was increasingly occupied by so-called *arrendires* in exchange for their labour. The *arrendire* is a peasant who, in exchange for a plot of virgin land, is obliged to work a number of days (5–15 per month) without remuneration on the land cultivated for the landlord. It often happens that the *arrendire* leases out part of his plot to an *allegado* who helps him fulfil the service to the landlord. The *allegado* in turn may have a *habilitado*, *agregado*, or *manipure*, a peon or manual labourer, in his service. Although the Constitution of 1933 prohibits work without remuneration (Article 55), such forms of servitude continued in La Convención as well as in other areas. In the Convención valley there were about 4,000 *arrendires*, with 12,000 *allegados* and an unknown number of day-labourers – altogether about 60,000 people.

Still, in La Convención the peasants were in a relatively favourable position, compared with other areas. The valley

forms part of the higher *selva* and most inhabitants came
the area during the last few decades as migrants, or pioneei.
They became *arrendires* on the large haciendas of mostly
virgin land but were able, after a number of years of work,
to improve their income considerably by the cultivation of
coffee and other tropical or subtropical cash crops. The
obligations of *arrendires* to work a number of days per week
on the owner's land became increasingly burdensome, specially when the *hacendados*, in view of the growing economic
independence of their *arrendires*, started to increase their demands, or tried to evict them.

By 1952 the peasants of one hacienda had already com-
bined to hire a lawyer who could formulate a protest and
represent them at the labour inspector's office. In the next
few years, peasants of other *haciendas* followed this example
and started to band together and organize unions. The protests were mainly concerned with the number of days worked
for the landowner, the excessive working hours per day compared with the legally established working day, and the free
sale of crops without intervention of the *hacendado*. In 1958,
eight of these newly formed unions joined together in the
Federación Provincial de Campesinos de la Convención y
Lares. The estate where the movement developed most
strongly and where the conditions were particularly bad was
Huadquiña, of which the haciendas Santa Rosa and Chaupimayo formed part. The entire property, one of several belonging to the same family, was over 100,000 hectares
according to conservative estimates. What created most resentment and hostility among the peasants in Chaupimayo
were the abuses of the landlord and the way he tried to show
and confirm his overwhelming power, for example, by flog-
ging peasants who were not servile enough. As a response to
this situation the peasant union was formed. Its secretary-
general, Andrés González, was originally from another part
of the area, which he had fled after a violent encounter with

his landlord. When the union was formed in Huadquiña, a Ministerial Resolution prohibiting the *arrendires* and *allegados* from forming syndicates made it possible to declare the union illegal. Consequently the main leaders were jailed for two years. During this period Andrés González became acquainted with Hugo Blanco, an agronomist from Cuzco, who had earlier been active as a labour organizer and Trotskyist political agitator and who was in prison for that reason. They became friends, and González took Hugo Blanco as an *allegado* on his plot in Chaupimayo when they were set free, after a hunger strike in 1959.

The union work was resumed and the first list of demands included : (1) that the union should be free to build a school and hire a teacher; (2) that the landlord should give receipts for the days of unpaid work accomplished each month; (3) that there should be proper payment for improvements, such as coffee plants, if a peasant were to leave or be evicted; (4) that the landlord should let the peasants use some days of obligatory labour to build bridges across the streams; (5) that there should be a first-aid box on the estate; (6) that clothes and utensils which the overseers had taken from the peasants should be returned; (7) that the landlord should supply the peasants with tools and food during days of unpaid work.

The landlord's answer to these demands was an effort to evict the leaders. The peasants responded with a refusal to perform the unpaid work. When police came to dislodge the peasants they found them prepared to defend their homes. This was the beginning of a large-scale movement.

Hugo Blanco soon became his union's representative to the local federation and helped in the formation of new syndicates in other places of the valley. He began to establish his name as an effective organizer. Care was taken that in the unions the *arrendires* as well as the *allegados* and the day-labourers participated, so as to avoid internal divisions. In 1960 strikes were organized in the haciendas Paccha Grande,

Chaucamayo and Chaupimayo to demand better treatment and the end of abuses. The strike meant that the peasants refused to fulfil the days of unpaid work on the lands of the estate used by the landlord. This had the advantage of allowing them to work more on their own plots. For the landlords it meant serious problems, particularly during the harvest periods. The tactics were successful and spread rapidly through the area, particularly during 1961 and 1962. Many more syndicates were formed and by the end of 1961 there were forty-two unions on strike in La Convención. It was difficult to do anything official against the strike, since the unpaid services were not allowed by the Constitution. At the end of December 1961 a general strike on all haciendas was announced and made a great impact. As a result the government of President Manuel Prado issued a decree on 24 April 1962 which abolished the obligations of unpaid labour in the area.

In the meantime, in 1961, the Federación Departamental de Campesinos y Comunidades del Cuzco had been formed with 214 sections, but a split soon occurred within the movement. Hugo Blanco and many of the newer unions wanted a radical land reform, brought about if necessary by the occupation of the haciendas, a tactic which could lead to violence if the landowners opposed. The older leaders were less ambitious in their requests. In the election for Secretary-General of the Federación Departamental Blanco received a majority, but the leaders of some twenty peasant unions refused to follow him and walked out. It was in that period, mid-1962, that Blanco became known, in many newspapers, as a Castro-type guerrilla leader. The press magnified the reputation of Blanco to legendary proportions, and thus obscured the emergence of a strong movement based on concrete demands.

Blanco encouraged in Chaupimayo – the estate where he lived – the building of a school, the hiring of a teacher by the union, the building of roads and similar community projects.

A certain revolutionary exaltation existed: alcoholic drinks were forbidden and union meetings were held daily. Chaupimayo also became the base at which several training courses gave instruction on agrarian reform to 150 peasant leaders from all over the area. It seems that at a later stage instruction in armed self-defence formed part of these courses. The idea behind this was that the peasants needed to form small militia groups in order to protect themselves and their wives and daughters against despoliation and the abuses of the landlords and to achieve effective political power. Contrary to the tactics of the guerrilla groups which operated in some areas of Peru, these militia groups strongly emphasized self-defence. It was stressed that this was only one aspect of the syndicate's activities, directed towards the elimination of the landlords' power. The publicity given to Blanco was due partly to the fact that in May 1962 a group of Trotskyist political activists who had robbed two banks and used part of the money to support the peasant movement in La Convención had been captured. The relationship between Blanco's movement and activities in Lima or elsewhere was probably the reason behind the order for his arrest in mid-1962, which forced him to go into hiding in his area. Because of the protection given by the peasants he was relatively safe there.

The peasant mobilization went on and became, partly as a result of the strong opposition of the landlords, more and more radical. The decree of April 1962 abolishing unpaid labour was not sufficient to calm down the movement. The most radical policy promoted by Blanco among the unions at that time was the occupation of haciendas. Later Blanco explained that this was to be part of an overall revolutionary strategy to win political power for the peasants and workers, beginning in the rural areas. A first stage of the strategy was the refusal to render the unpaid services or to pay the rent. The second stage was to start work on the idle lands of the hacienda. As planned, the third stage was to occupy those lands worked for the owner. Also his house and other establishments were to be put to collective use. If the landlord worked his property efficiently and had not committed abuses his property would be respected. Some landlords, such as the owner of the Huadquiña estate, known for their abusiveness were chased away and not allowed to return. The argument of the peasants was that they had long since paid with unremunerated work for the value of the land they now occupied. In some estates the peasants built temporary huts to indicate that the land was now theirs.

The occupations were organized simultaneously in different places and carried out in a coordinated way so that an effective power would be developed in competition with that of the landlords. These occupations went on during several months of 1962, particularly in October. Many landlords left the area at that time. The peasants formed armed groups to defend the lands they had occupied or which they possessed but from which they were threatened with eviction. That practically no violence or destruction was involved in such activities is surprising, when seen in the light of the treatment which the peasants generally had to suffer.

Shortly after this some landlords tried to divide the peasant movement by creating 'free unions', and repressive acts by the police caused the escalation of peasant resistance leading to considerable violence. Troops were moved into the area, and it is impossible to unravel the mutual accusations of provocation for the violence. The incidents culminated in a massacre in Chaullay, in which according to official sources five peasants were killed; according to eye-witnesses scores of people fell. A few days later, in January 1963, hundreds of peasant leaders and lawyers in the area were captured. However, the occupations of lands could not reversed, and the only way to calm the movement appeared to be to legalize the new situation.

The military government which had overthrown the Prado

regime in mid-1962 issued a special land reform decree for the valleys of Convención and Lares (No. 14444, March 1963), which recognized the *de facto* control by the *arrendires* of their holdings. To obtain a legal title they would have to pay in twenty years. Priorities were established for expropriation : (1) the estates operated with the help of *arrendires* and *allegados*; (2) those which were not well farmed; and (3) those which constituted an excessive concentration of property.

Hugo Blanco was aware that the movement he led had come to a head too early, before other areas of Peru had been sufficiently organized for the revolutionary effort to spread all over the country. This made it possible for the military government to check the revolt and keep it within the limits of the Convención area through land distribution and military action. With the arrival in the area of many troops, it became increasingly difficult for Hugo Blanco to be kept hidden. He was captured in May 1963 and sent to prison in Arequipa. He was sentenced to twenty-five years, for the killing of three policemen.

The agrarian movement continued to be strong, and probably Blanco's instructions were even more faithfully followed than usual, since his imprisonment made him appear a martyr. This was noted by an observer who visited the area in early 1964 and attended a peasant mass meeting in Quillabamba.

All this happened while the legitimacy of the national government was severely in doubt because of a military takeover in the middle of 1962, after elections in which Haya de la Torre, the candidate not approved by the military, had won the most votes. In early 1963, while the country was still under military rule, there was another presidential election campaign in Peru, in which the candidates made firm promises regarding land reform. According to eye-witnesses, one candidate, Belaunde Terry, distributed small bags of earth among the peasants as an advance on the lands he would give after becoming president. Belaunde Terry won the elections and became president in mid-1963. It is obvious that a good deal of political agitation resulted from the promises made by those who later formed the government. Peasant pressure in Peru, apart from that generated in the Convención valley, was partly a result of the political competition during the election campaigns of 1962 and 1963. This pressure was not organized systematically into groups following national directives (as happened in Venezuela), but was mainly organized locally.

The CIDA study of Peru noted that by mid-1963 there were altogether about 300,000 peasants actively pressuring through land invasions for the reforms which had been promised by the various politicians in their campaigns. To a large extent the politicians had responded to strongly felt needs and grievances existing among the peasants about their formerly communal lands which they had lost over the years, and which were either in litigation or under consideration for 'recovery' by the peasant communities. Only in a few areas, such as in the Central Highlands in the departments of Junín and Pasco, did peasant pressure appear to be sufficiently coordinated and organized to achieve a lasting impact similar to that in La Convención. It was in those areas that the land reform programme was initiated and land was distributed. A great number of less effectively organized activities took place in other areas in those years.

The movement created by the peasant federations in Cuzco, Pasco and Junín spread in late 1963 to other areas where local organizations and federations had been formed. During the following months many invasions took place, sometimes accompanied by acts of violence. Several parts of the country, particularly the coastal zone close to Lima, and the departments of Piura in the north and Cuzco in the south, became the scene of such activities.

After the Minister of the Interior had been severely criticized by representatives of the landowning class for tolerating the invasions, the government's policy changed. At the end of 1963 a new minister was appointed and the police started to repress the peasant movements. This policy resulted in considerable violence. In the densely populated Sicuani area, in the department of Cuzco, the roads were blocked by the peasants to prevent the entrance of the police force. In the ensuing battle twenty peasants were killed.

However, for the most part the invasions were not violent in the sense that they led to intentional destruction of human life or goods. Generally the lives, houses and other belongings of the landlords were safe, as long as negotiations were started and no efforts made to dislodge the peasants or their cattle from the parts they had occupied. One landlord who had killed seven peasants in an encounter, however, was not allowed to return to his estate.

In some areas the organized invasions reached proportions that came close to what Bolivia had experienced in 1952–3. Descriptions of the occurrences in those areas indicate that the *patrones* were practically obliged to come to an agreement with the local organizations and federations. If this was done on a basis of mutual agreement and compromise, the landlords were generally respected.

After January 1964, however, the government did not tolerate or channel this process, as in Bolivia, but attempted to repress it. A considerable army or police force was stationed in several of the urban centres in the agitated areas and the leaders of the organizations were captured and imprisoned.

In addition to this, the agrarian reform law of 21 May 1964 indicated that invaded lands would not be used for the reform programme. This had the effect that many of the invaded estates were disoccupied: in Cuzco alone, the peasants left 104 of the 114 occupied estates peacefully. Another reason for the abandonment of invaded lands was that the most agitated regions, such as the departments of Pasco, Junín and Cuzco, were immediately declared agrarian reform areas. A great number of technicians of the Oficina Nacional de Reforma Agraria (ONRA) were sent to establish themselves in those areas, giving the peasants the impression that a solution to their problem was close. The two huge estates where most of the invasions occurred, in the departments of Pasco and Junín, the Algolan estate and the Cerro de Pasco Corporation, soon became part of the agrarian reform programme.

It was indicated by several local informants that the actual beginning of the reform project, the distribution of the plots to the *comunidades* for exploitation through 'communal enterprises', occurred in a period when a group of guerrillas headed by Guillermo Lobatón, which formed part of a campaign started in early 1965 by leftist groups to overthrow the government by armed force, came close to the area.

It seems that there was no organizational relationship between the peasant invasions in the years 1960–63 and the guerrilla groups that operated in Peru in 1965. In the Convención and Cerro de Pasco areas, where strong peasant organizations existed, the pending implementation of agrarian reform was probably accelerated when guerrilla groups appeared in the neighbourhood. Elsewhere, in the Satipo region for example, peasant organizations were completely repressed because of the presence of guerrillas. The pretext used by the military authorities was that the local unions, affiliates of the moderate Christian-Democrat labour movement in Peru, had contacts with the guerrillas. One top leader was assassinated, another imprisoned and tortured; and several hamlets of organized squatters, disputing lands with large landowners, were destroyed. The relationship between the guerrillas and the peasant organizations remains unclear. For example, the guerrilla group headed by Luis de la Puente Uceda which operated in the Convención area in 1965 apparently did not find much response among the peasants.

The guerrilla forces were all repressed in 1965 by the armed forces. The peasant movement in La Convención and Pasco and Junín, as such, survived and – temporarily it seems – withdrew into non-political activities related to the agrarian reform programme carried out in the area.

### 3. THE NORTH-EAST OF BRAZIL: PEASANT LEAGUES AND COMPETING ORGANIZATIONS

The growth between 1955 and 1964 of the *Ligas Camponeses* (Peasant Leagues) in the north-east of Brazil, mainly in the states of Pernambuco and Paraiba, should be seen as a consequence of the overall situation in which the peasantry lived. The activities of the Leagues were mainly concentrated in an area relatively close to Recife, the state capital, with good communications. Because of the low sugar prices during the thirties several sugar plantations (*engenhos*) in this area had been rented out by the owners, who lived in the city, to peasants, who cultivated fruits and cereals to supply the city. In cases where the landowner cultivated part of his estate himself, generally through an administrator, his tenants had to render free services, called *cambão* or *condicão*, or to work for wages lower than the prevailing rate. When sugar prices went up again during and after the Second World War landlords tried to evict the peasants from the plots they had been cultivating and to transform the estates again into sugar plantations. The peasants lived in great insecurity and paid, in money, kind and/or services, a rent which was per year almost half the commercial value of the plot of land. It was in one of these *engenhos* that the *Ligas Camponeses* had their origin.

Peasant Leagues had existed in Brazil for a good number

of years. The first Leagues were formed in the forties by the Communist Party in several parts of the country. One of the participants in this campaign was José dos Prazeres, a peasant's son who had worked on the land in his youth, but later went to work in town and managed to become literate. He became involved in the anarcho-syndicalist labour movement and tried to go as a volunteer to support the peasants in the Mexican revolution of 1910. He landed in jail, however, before the recruiting ship had left Recife. He later worked as a tram-conductor and became a member of the Communist Party. He participated in the Party's campaign to organize peasant leagues after 1945. When the Party was outlawed in 1947, the Leagues which had been formed were practically all destroyed by police repression, except the one in Iputinga, on the outskirts of Recife. Prazeres left the Communist Party and dedicated himself to peasant organization. In 1955, in the *engenho* Galileia in the municipality of Victória de Santo Antão where he worked, he helped to found the Sociedade Agricola e Pecuaria dos Plantadores de Pernambuco (SAPPP).

The main purpose of the Sociedade was to establish through contributions in cash or in kind a small fund which could be used to help the peasants to avoid eviction because of failure to pay their debts to the landlord. The rent which the peasants had to pay was extravagantly high, about 6,000 cruzeiros per hectare per year, and as the value of the land was 10,000 to 15,000 cruzeiros per hectare, the owner received as much as the value of the rented land after about two years of rent payment. In Galileia this was the situation of about 150 families, who rented altogether about 500 hectares. The *sociedade* hoped to use its fund to buy the land from the owner, so that in the future the peasants could avoid the extravagant rents and the accompanying danger of being evicted if they were not able to pay them. In order to avoid the repression which earlier Leagues had encountered, the purpose of the new society included a range of civic activities, such as the cooperative buying of coffins, and the owner of the *engenho* was chosen as honorary president. He soon resigned, however, apparently under pressure from his son and other landowners in the area, and the society started to meet with serious difficulties. Prazeres then looked for support among urban professionals and political figures of different tendencies. This support was particularly needed when the son of the landlord wanted to evict the peasants who were members of the association, and use the land which they had been cultivating for years for cattle-breeding, so as to get rid of the 'problem'. The peasants had been working those lands for over fifteen years. When the landlord's son went ahead with his plan, the *sociedade* sought the help of Francisco Julião de Paula, a lawyer in Recife, and state deputy for the small Socialist Party. The leaders of the society then succeeded in making the owner bring a suit for eviction against them in the courts.

In January 1955 Julião helped the society to gain legal status as a civil association with mutual benefit purposes, with headquarters in Recife and several municipal branches or 'delegations'. Such branches had been formed in Tamatamirin and in Surubin. Soon the groups were called Leagues. The society was registered as a civil association and not as a labour union because the problems which the peasants had to face were generally related to the contractual conditions of land tenure, which fall under the civil code rather than the labour legislation.

As part of the campaign to make the Leagues known and respected, mass meetings or marches were held in Recife. In 1955, 3,000 peasants marched to the Legislative Assembly when a session on land reform was going on. On 1 May 1956, 600 peasants and workers demonstrated together in Recife.

Francisco Julião came himself from a landholder's family,

his father owning a relatively small estate of 280 hectares in Bom Jardin, managed by one of Julião's six brothers. Forty workers were employed on this estate. Among the first Leagues was the one formed in Bom Jardin which was at that time the only estate where meetings could be held. It became a centre of agitation in the area. On other private properties meetings were forbidden and had to be held secretly. At that time there was a great deal of agitation against the Leagues. Talk about agrarian reform was branded as subversive and on one occasion in 1956 Julião was imprisoned.

One way to protect the Leagues, which initially led an almost clandestine life, was for them to be visited frequently by state deputies who, with their parliamentary immunity and status, could prevent police attacks. The urban supporters of the society formed a steering council which could defend it at the level of the state capital. For that purpose the society had been conceived as a regional organization covering the whole state of Pernambuco with local base organizations or nuclei. Having a seat in the state capital and a group of supporters to defend it at that level was a guarantee of survival for the peasant organization as a whole. It was also juridically an advantage to have a regional organization legally recognized and registered. As local nuclei were created they could obtain legal status without delay. This method of creating a regional organization with an increasing number of local nuclei, rather than of creating local organizations and bringing them together into a federation, proved to be a great asset. It was the reverse of the tactics which had formerly been applied with little success.

The movement benefited considerably from the wide publicity given to the problems of north-east Brazil at the Congress for the Salvation of the North-East, which was held on 20–7 August 1955 in Recife. There were 1,600 delegates from the nine states of the north-east representing all strata of society – labour unions, educational institutions, government, business, industry and also peasants. Representatives of the Leagues participated, particularly in the 200-member committee on land problems. The backward agrarian situation prevailing in the north-east was criticized, and a declaration in favour of agrarian reform adopted. This Congress and some similar meetings in the following years led to the creation of a Committee for the Development of the North-East out of which SUDENE (Superintendencia de Desenvolvimiento do Nord-este) grew.

In September 1955, the Leagues demonstrated their existence by attending the First Congress of Peasants of Pernambuco, organized with the support of FAO president Josue de Castro. José dos Prazeres was elected president of the SAPPP, the society to which all Leagues officially belonged. The congress ended with a mass demonstration of several thousand peasants through the streets of Recife, which made a deep impression on urban public opinion, and gave the peasants, possibly for the first time, a sense of their power.

Through such activities the Leagues emerged from the isolation in which the landowners of the area had tried to keep them. The commercial and industrial groups which, allied with representatives of workers and peasants, had promoted the Congress for the Salvation of the North-East soon gained a victory in the elections, and obtained for the first time a mayor for Recife who was not the representative of the conservative landowners' interests. The landed interests quickly started a campaign against this new alliance, by promoting a tax reform which would be harmful to small commerce and industry. This provoked a stronger unity in favour of reforms. During the struggle between the opposing interest groups, the Peasant Leagues suffered considerably particularly in the beginning of 1956. Many peasant and labour leaders were imprisoned. Later during the year and again at the beginning of 1957, a general strike took place which was supported by the Peasant Leagues and helped to increase political awareness among the agricultural workers and peasants.

In 1958 a state governor was elected who was an industrialist and the candidate of the alliance of interests opposing the traditional landed elite. The repressive climate which had existed particularly in the rural areas changed, and it was under those circumstances that in 1959 the Peasant League of Galileia, still litigating with the landowner in the courts, was able to obtain the distribution of the land of the estate. This happened after huge peasant demonstrations in the streets, and even in the legislative assembly of Pernambuco, exerted pressure for the approval of the expropriation of the estate as proposed by the socialist deputy Carlos Luis de Andrade.

The Leagues gained considerable prestige through this victory, although the peasants of Galileia lost their interest in the agrarian struggle after their own success. Other Leagues became the centre of the movement. Several of their leaders had a chance to visit Cuba in 1959 and 1960 and thus became acquainted with a radical agrarian reform. During those years the movement spread through the states of Pernambuco (altogether in twenty-six municipalities) and Paraiba and even beyond. The mutual help of experienced peasant organizers such as José dos Prazeres and urban political and labour leaders led to an effective agitation and formation strategy.

The strategy used in the formation of the Peasant Leagues included the following points:

1. The great flexibility of structure. Since the *Liga* was legally a civil association, once a *Liga* existed at the state level, in each community or municipality, a *delegação* could be founded. The word *delegação* was used on purpose because it was the same as the word for a local police station and to have their own *delegação* would help to overcome the peasants' tremendous fear of the police. In order to form a local nucleus, or *delegação*, it was sufficient for a group of thirty or

forty people to approve the statutes of the *Liga* (at the central level) and elect a board.

2. The policy of starting to work with small farmers, tenants, sharecroppers and in general those peasants who have a stronger economic basis than the agricultural wage workers. The last category had very little means to support the movement, and nothing to fall back upon when there was need to resist. Since many agricultural workers were seasonal, they could not be counted upon in the building-up of a locally established organization. The workers could join and strengthen the movement, but it was firmly based on those who had at least a guaranteed subsistence.

3. Related to these two points is the fact that, before the passage of new labour legislation in 1963, a small peasant had a stronger position within the context of the civil law than the worker had under the labour law. If tenants or sharecroppers refused to leave the land when told to by the landowners (as frequently happened), the waiting time while an eviction suit was going on at the court was no loss to the peasants, who continued to cultivate their plots, and thus could carry on litigating in the court for years until they had won their case. Agricultural workers below the subsistence level soon found it difficult to keep up a strike.

4. The technique of winning the peasants for the *Ligas* was based on the highest possible degree of identification with their mentality so as to win their confidence. This was done mainly through struggling on their side to win cases against the pressures of the landowners. In the process of identification and winning confidence, the well-known *violeiros*, popular and peasant poets and singers, played an important role. The struggle kept on for years, and this, together with the intimate contact needed to wield the support from the communities, helped strong feelings of solidarity to develop.

5. Publicity, especially of cases in which the landowners violently and illegally opposed the organization (as when the

peasant leader of Sapé, João Pedro Teixeira, was assassinated), gave the movement a strong impetus. In a later stage the *Ligas* had their own weekly paper. Urban supporters including lawyers, workers and students helped to spread the Leagues. They often tried to find popular leaders in a local community and discover what were the strongly felt grievances. Many of the founders of local branches were peasants who had got in touch with the already existing Leagues and their leaders.

Soon the movement spread beyond the state of Pernambuco. The Leagues were brought to the state of Paraiba in 1959 by João Pedro Teixeira, a peasant of Sapé, who had spent some time in Pernambuco. In 1963, the League in Sapé had about 10,000 members. Sapé had in common with the area of Victória de Santo Antão, where the first League had been formed, that the majority of the peasants, generally rural wage workers, had a plot for subsistence. The town of Sapé had good communications with the capital of Paraiba, João Pessoa.

The first activities of this League were to claim indemnification in the courts in cases where peasants had been evicted. It was at this stage that landowners started to prohibit peasants who rented a plot from planting fruit trees or other permanent crops. Also, the repair of the houses inhabited by the peasants was prohibited in some cases. The first leader, João Pedro Teixeira, was assassinated in April 1962 by henchmen of the landlord. He had protested against eviction without proper compensation for the improvements he had made. This happened when the estate had changed ownership, and the new owner wanted to get rid of him. (One of the most difficult obstacles in the formation of the *Ligas* was the threat of assassination of leaders, particularly since on several occasions this threat was carried out. Traditionally the landlords had private policemen, so-called *capangas*, in their service to do these jobs. However, with the slowly increasing strength of the movement the peasants started to fight back and at times *capangas* or even landlords were killed in such acts.)

The impact of the agitation and growth of the Peasant Leagues became particularly visible during the First National Congress of Peasants and Agricultural Workers in Belo Horizonte, 15–17 November 1961. A number of agricultural workers' organizations which had been in the meantime founded in other parts of the country participated in this congress. The most important were the Union of Agricultural Workers of Brazil (ULTAB) with headquarters in São Paulo, and the Movement of Peasants without Land (MASTER) of Rio Grande do Sul. The President of the Republic and many high authorities, including the members of the National Agrarian Reform Commission, were present. There was a strong delegation from the Peasant Leagues, which made a tremendous impact by their radical demand for land. While most organizations present had a moderate reform programme, the vociferous way the peasants of the north-east, the poorest-looking delegation in the congress, demanded radical reform won over the congress.

The movement started to gain support from more important urban circles. Several informants have indicated that the campaign for the formation of Leagues and, for example, the periodical *Liga*, which appeared in Rio de Janeiro and propagandized the work of the Leagues and the need for agrarian reform at the national level, were financed partly by São Paulo industrialists. These groups had an interest in agrarian reform, because a more equal distribution of income in the rural areas would considerably increase the market possibilities for industrial products. Meanwhile other groups began to fear the *Ligas'* growing strength. Even before the congress of Belo Horizonte the Catholic Church in the north-east had started to organize peasant unions in order to counteract the increasing and radicalizing influence of the Peasant Leagues.

An important element in the campaign for unionization

in Rio Grande do Norte was the so-called 'conscientization'. This was done through the Basic Education Movement, MEB, promoted by the General Assembly of Bishops since 1962. Radio schools were used, with the assistance of local promotors, to bring the peasants awareness of the need to change the paternalistic social structure. MEB tried to introduce new ideas in many different ways. One of its methods was a form of literacy teaching which at the same time helped people to become aware of their social situation and of the need to change it. This method is named after its inventor and promoter, Paulo Freire.

In March 1963 a new Rural Labour Statute facilitated the formation of unions, and many of the Peasant Leagues then transformed themselves into unions. The Leagues often won the respect of the peasants because they took the initiative in striking, while the church unions signed agreements with the landlords. The landlords themselves, by breaking their promises to the church unions but yielding to the Leagues' threats of violence, indirectly helped them.

Competition for the leadership became more severe as more church groups, political groups, government agencies and other interests tried to become involved in the movement to create peasant organizations. Under the Rural Labour Statute, rural unionization fell under the terms of the Consolidation of the Labour Law of 1943. This implied that in one municipality there could exist only one peasant union. A consequence of this was that within a municipality the competing factions had to fight for control within the only existing union.

In June 1963, shortly after the promulgation of the Rural Labour Statute, the Ministry of Labour and SUPRA (the institute designated to be in charge of agrarian reform) jointly started a peasant unionization campaign. Its main promoter, Father Francisco Lage Pessoa, stressed that President Goulart needed an organized peasantry to obtain a majority in parliament. For that reason the organization started in the more densely populated areas close to the cities, where important sectors of the electorate lived. In about six months 2,000 unions were created with between 50 (the legal minimum) and 3,000 members each. Students, often radical Catholics of Accão Popular, helped in the campaign. It became clear that the peasants had picked up the idea of land reform. In most places proposals for moderate improvements brought forward by the organizers were overruled by the peasants demanding land.

In the north-east, unions were formed where previously they did not exist, causing the Peasant Leagues to lose some of their impact. At times they worked with the syndicates, for example in the organization of the massive strike of 200,000 peasant workers in November 1963, which brought to the peasants all the benefits required by law, such as legally established minimum wages and working hours.

These continued efforts gave additional strength to the movement but, with the *coup d'état* of April 1964, the whole situation was reversed and repression started. Leaders were imprisoned and tortured and the government interfered with many unions including those of the church. Most of the unions' gains, such as minimum wages and working hours, were undone.

## 4. COLOMBIA: A CASE OF ILLEGITIMACY AND VIOLENCE

As we have seen from the cases of Mexico, Bolivia and Venezuela, there is a close relationship between the existence of strong peasant organizations and agrarian reform. In Colombia agrarian reform legislation has been related to unstructured peasant movements that started as a reaction to the illegal practices, intransigence and violence of the landed elite. As yet there are practically no structured peasant organizations in Colombia. But the study of the spontaneous peasant movements gives some insight into the possibilities for peasant organization.

In the twenties and thirties the land tenure issue came up partly as a result of the introduction of banana – or in some areas coffee – plantations which led to the proletarization of many peasants. Experienced peasant leaders such as Juan de la Cruz Varela, together with urban organizers, started an effective agrarian movement, particularly in the Sumapaz area, not far from Bogotá. An important issue that radicalized the peasants in some places, such as Viotá, was the demand of the coffee workers to have the right to cultivate coffee on the small plots which they were allowed to use for their subsistence. The landlords were afraid that this right would lead to greater independence of the peasants and refused. The peasants were thus forcefully awakened to the land tenure issue.

It was not only in the areas of the coffee estates that the landowners' resistance to gradual change created opposition among the peasants. In several neighbouring regions the landlords tried to assert their real or alleged property rights aggressively. This was most frequently done by evicting tenants or squatters with the support of the police or the armed forces. Many local battles resulted. This happened particularly in those areas which had become more accessible through road building, and where – at the cost of the tax-payer – the value of landed property increased. Tolima, Cundinamarca and the Cauca valley were such areas, and they later became the principal scene of the guerrilla and *bandolero* activities summarized under the name *la violencia*.

In an official investigation of the problem of boundaries and properties it was noted that surprisingly large tracts of land were in the hands of private persons who had taken them from the national domain without legal title. In the departments of Cundinamarca and Tolima alone, authorizations to start lawsuits against such persons covered about 500,000 hectares.

Partly as a reaction to growing peasant unrest in some of these areas, and to the Liberal government's attempt to gain control over them, Law 200 regarding agrarian reform was promulgated in 1936. This law provided that private lands which had not been cultivated by their owners for more than ten years would return to public property. The law had enhanced the hopes of the peasants of getting land, since certain guarantees were included for squatters who had worked certain lands for two years or more. However, a result of the law was that many peasants were evicted from the plots they had cultivated (with or without compensation for the improvements they had made). Many landlords, believing that tenants or sharecroppers would claim the rights guaranteed in that law, tried even harder to get rid of them.

The complications of the law, and the way it was often interpreted by the landlords, had a most frustrating effect on the peasants. Invasions became more frequent, and their legitimacy was always debatable.

It increasingly occurred, however, that the peasants' activities in defence of their own interests were branded as 'violence' and then made the pretext for violent intervention by the police, the army or private bands of the landowners. Violence occurred particularly in those regions where most injustices had been committed by landowners, with help from the police, the army or their own bands, and where, as a result, a climate of lawlessness prevailed. The land tenure problems became part of a conflict between the Liberal and Conservative Parties that flared up in 1947 and extended rapidly after the assassination of the Liberal presidential candidate with leftist tendencies, Jorge Eliecer Gaitán, on 1 April 1948 in Bogotá.

Another issue which continued to cause violent reaction was the despoliation of indigenous groups by the landholders, provoking efforts to recover lost lands. This happened for example in Chaparral, department of Tolima, where two haciendas which had formerly been indigenous *resguardos* were invaded in 1938. The peasants on such occasions expressed the belief that they were acting in accordance with the law. But the despoliation of indigenous groups continued. In 1949 the Troche Indians in the Marquetalia area were forced to sell their lands. It was in this area and in the region of Viotá, where the peasants had strong organizations, that self-defence regions were established in those years. Later, some of these areas became internationally famous as 'independent republics'.

In most areas of Colombia violence raged in a very disorderly way, at times taking the form of mere banditry. In some periods it grew into a civil war between the opposing Liberal and Conservative Parties that used the more or less ignorant peasantry to fight out their party conflicts. Altogether, in a little over ten years 200,000 to 300,000 people were killed, but few or no concrete benefits were gained for the peasantry.

An interesting explanation of *la violencia* was given by the sociologist Father Camilo Torres. The lack of social mobility, and an increasing awareness of this lack among the rural population, created frustration and latent aggression, which at a certain stage became manifest because no constructive ways to overcome the situation were opened. One result of the whole experience of *la violencia* was a break in the *status quo*, in the sense that peasants became conscious of their power and lost a great part of their habitual feeling of inferiority. The peasants also lost respect for the traditional and rigid social structure, and a greater class consciousness or group solidarity has resulted. This seems to be similar to the effects provoked by the Chaco War in Bolivia.

Already in a few areas during the years of strife, the political parties initially responsible for the violence began to lose control over the peasantry. Peasants started to become aware of their own interests, which were different from those of either of the two parties. Later, when the leadership of the guerrilla groups fell into the hands of leaders of peasant background rather than party politicians (as in the Llanos), and when the first programmes proposing land reform were elaborated (the laws of the Llanos of 11 September 1952 and of 18 June 1953), the Liberal and Conservative Parties both felt simultaneously threatened and began to seek a coalition. The new government that then came to power under General Rojas Pinilla tried to appease the peasantry with promises of amnesty and land reform. However, after a short period of tranquillity Conservative opposition to the possible execution of these promises caused the violent struggle in the rural areas to flare up again.

Conservative Party adherents in southern Tolima, the Cauca valley and the department of Caldas started again to terrorize small towns into opposing and provoking difficulties for the Rojas Pinilla government. At the end of 1954, after the massacre of peasants, the Communist-led groups in Sumapaz, headed by the peasant leader Juan de la Cruz Varela, took again to guerrilla activities. In April 1955 the government sent ten to fifteen thousand soldiers with planes and tanks to Sumapaz, and broke the Communist defence line. Thousands of peasants fled to more isolated regions. Then, in the south of Tolima, Liberal-oriented peasants influenced by the Communist groups took up arms until the army took the defence zone by assault. The groups in the Llanos declared solidarity with the peasants of Sumapaz and Tolima in February 1957. In the 1955–7 period the struggle was more limited to certain specific areas than in the earlier periods and apparently became a confrontation between thousands of peasants and the army. Although generally in rhetorical terms, the peasants' proclamations in this period spoke of revolution and agrarian reform.

As a result of the large-scale military actions and the ousting of the Rojas Pinilla government, which was replaced by a Liberal-Conservative coalition, the struggle in the rural areas diminished from 1958 onwards. The need for important reforms in the agrarian structure, however, was forcefully brought to the attention of the nation.

One important result of the violence which swept the rural areas was that in December 1961 the government promulgated agrarian reform legislation (Law 135) and created an agency to apply the law, the Colombian Land Reform Institute (INCORA). The first project initiated by INCORA was in one of the most violence-ridden areas – Cunday, department of Tolima – an area where large coffee plantations and other estates had been neglected for years because of the violent activities. The few land reform projects initiated by INCORA during the following years generally also coincided with areas where trouble existed, mainly in the form of land invasions.

The Colombian government tried to repress and appease the peasants through both minor reforms and armed force. The repression was relatively successful, but since only very few effective reform measures have been carried out discontent will probably rise. Under proper guidance this discontent might well be channelled into a strong movement in favour of radical change or even open revolution – if no other ways of solving the existing conflicts are found. How frustration of orderly and legalized ways of radical agrarian change leads to an increasing potential for violent peasant action is shown by the developments during the last decades in Guatemala.

## 5. GUATEMALA: REFORM AND COUNTER-REFORM

As in Venezuela, peasant organization and agrarian reform in Guatemala were introduced from above by a reformist or populist government. When the reform started to become effective the government was overthrown by outside intervention. A counter-reform movement was initiated re-establishing the 'culture of repression'. From the Guatemalan case it becomes clear that frustrated reform efforts have a radicalizing effect on the traditional and repressed peasants. For an assessment of the organizational potential of peasants in Latin America the Guatemalan case is an important one.

In 1944, after many years of repressive dictatorship, the 'populist' Juan José Arévalo came to power. Labour unions, collective bargaining, minimum hours and similar measures were allowed and promoted. Peasant organizations began to form after the reform of the Labour Code in July 1948, which recognized for the first time the right of peasants to form unions.

Urban labour groups were the main promoters of the campaign to organize the peasants. Organization began and was most effective in the areas with better communications and where modernizing influences were stronger: this was in the areas close to Guatemala City and Esquintla. One factor favourable to the 'organizability' of rural workers in those areas was the frustrating effect of the presence of the United Fruit Company establishment.

In 1950, the National Peasant Federation of Guatemala, the CNCG, was founded with Leonardo Castillo Flores, an ex-teacher who became union organizer, and Amor Velasco de León, an agricultural worker with experience in Mexico, as its main leaders. Some 200 delegates representing four regional federations and 25 peasant unions participated in the founding of the CNCG. The movement grew rapidly under the presidency of Arévalo's successor, Jacobo Arbenz, elected in 1951. By 1954, it had, according to calculations made by Nathan Whetten, 1,500 active unions with 180,000–190,000 members. This was in spite of the fact that, on the one hand, some Communist groups were competing and, on the other, a number of Catholic priests tried to stop the peasants from joining by labelling the movement 'Communist'.

To support the agrarian reform law in May–June 1952, various peasant rallies were held in Guatemala City to pressure the Congress into action as well as to give the thousands of peasants brought in from the countryside a sense of participation in making the legislation which was to govern them. Provisions for the participation of peasant organizations in the execution of the land reform were included.

The agrarian reform law (Ley de Reforma Agraria, Decreto número 900) of 17 June 1952 was designed to liquidate idle latifundia property and to abolish all types of servitude. It provided for the expropriation of privately owned land which was not cultivated by the owner or on his behalf. No private land farmed by the owner or under his supervision was to be taken, and properties of less than 2 *caballerías* (90 hectares) would be respected, whether cultivated or not.

In some areas the local affiliates of the CNCG anticipated the passing of the reform law by publishing lists of landholders they considered to be eligible for expropriation. When the law was issued, they began to measure off these same lands. Because of the opposition of the landlords to the law, on occasions leading to violence, an amendment was included shortly after its promulgation punishing them with total expropriation without any indemnification. Although there was some unrest in certain areas, on the whole the reform process went with considerable speed and order.

CIDA has indicated that about 100,000 peasants benefited

from the reform in eighteen months. It has also noted that between January 1953 and June 1954 a little over 600,000 hectares were expropriated. This land represented sixteen per cent of the country's total idle lands in private hands which could be available for cultivation. Production of foodstuffs went up considerably in 1953–4. However, the fact that 83,000 hectares of unused land belonging to the United Fruit Company were expropriated, with reimbursement only for the declared tax value of the land, created an international problem, which was to contribute to the overthrow of the Arbenz government in 1954.

On the fall of the Arbenz regime the landlords began the *de facto* recovery of the lands which they had lost. The peasants who had received land through the reform programme were dispossessed, at times by force, or they fled, causing considerable unrest in the rural areas. Although the new government several times urged the landlords not to take vengeance on the peasants who had benefited from the land reform, a good deal of violence did occur. The General Confederation of Labour compiled a list of 217 peasants assassinated during the first few weeks after the take-over. Following these and similar events, violence has continued in several regions of Guatemala to this day.

The CIDA report noted that the persecution of those who had participated in the reforms or worked in rural unions resulted in distrust and passive resistance in much of the rural sector. In some areas, in spite of severe repression, or possibly because of it, peasants gave considerable support to guerrilla groups. A young army officers' revolt on 13 November 1960 was crushed but the peasants offered support to some of the officers who had fled across the border and called upon them to start an armed struggle for land. Such a struggle was started in February 1962 in the Izabal region and is still going on today.

# CHAPTER 6

# Some Important Factors Regarding the Formation of Peasant Organizations

In the first three chapters it was demonstrated that the distrust and 'resistance to change' of peasants, as it exists all over Latin America, is not as such a hindrance to the creation of effective representative peasant organizations. On the contrary, distrust and 'resistance to change' make a useful starting point for the creation of strong peasant interest groups, provided that these groups are directed towards forms of change that are radical enough to satisfy the basic peasant demands. In general this implies that these interest groups are formed in opposition to, or in conflict with, the vested interests of the large estate owners. Since in most of Latin America the traditional hacienda system, and the 'culture of repression' accompanying it, are maintained up to the present, the prevailing climate is favourable to the formation of radical peasant organizations. That relatively few such peasant interest groups have been formed in Latin America is due to the absence of a number of factors that seem to be crucial for the creation of such organizations.

The few effective and large-scale peasant movements that there have been in Latin America have a number of factors in common that seem to be necessary for the formation of a successful peasant organization:

1. In addition to an overall 'organizability' of peasants, implied in their resistance to the 'culture of repression', there are certain specific conditions of frustration, generally related

to modernizing influences, that are favourable to the actual initiation of a peasant protest action leading to effective organization. Contact with urban and other modernizing forces comes out as a crucial factor in this 'organizability'.

2. In the actual process of formation, an important first step is the creation of awareness among the peasants of their basic interests and grievances, and of the possibility that united action can be undertaken to defend those interests – even if this implies a conflict with the traditional landed elite.

3. In order to bring the peasants into an active struggle for their own interests, the availability of strong or charismatic local leaders is crucial. Such leaders have to fulfil certain roles, such as inspiring confidence and courage, that make it easier for the peasants to withdraw from and even oppose the influence of the traditional patronage of their landlords.

4. Support from educated urban allies who can help in the building-up of a well-structured large-scale organization is another crucial factor for success. Peasants' organizations generally become effective only when they cover at least a whole geographic region.

5. In the dynamics of the formation of a peasant organization, the kinds of demands, and the means used to pressure for their fulfilment, are very important. In general one can note an escalation of demands as well as of the means of pressure. This is a result of the intransigence and sometimes violent opposition of the landlords. While starting with concrete and minor issues, and using strictly institutionalized ways of making their demands, peasant organizations have seen themselves obliged to rely on more and more radical approaches in order to reach their legitimate goals. These often include forms of civil disobedience and sometimes even violence. Since the land reform issue is generally the main reason for peasant discontent, peaceful occupation of unused

or badly used parts of large estates has been an important means in the peasant struggle, to which considerable attention has to be given.

## 1. SOME COMMON FACTORS AS CONDITIONS FOR EFFECTIVE PEASANT ORGANIZATIONS

It is clear from a comparison of the various organized movements that they all occurred in areas where modernizing influences of some kind had been at work. The striking fact about these influences, however, was that they brought frustration to the majority of the peasants rather than improvement, or left them at the margin of the benefits of development. The expansion of the sugar estates, at the cost of the land and the independence of the communal farmers in the state of Morelos, Mexico, where Zapata operated, is a clear case in point. The local population was practically forced to find a living working on the sugar hacienda lands which formerly belonged to them.

In Ucureña, Cochabamba, peasants who through organized effort had achieved some degree of liberation from traditional feudal obligations were forced back into the old system, which had become increasingly burdensome. They were thrown off the land they had rented together. Frequently, once a few peasants had achieved a certain independence through buying a small plot, others who were attracted by this example were punished or frustrated when organizing to obtain the same.

In La Convención in Peru, the increased economic progress of the local peasants, and the greater independence from the large landowners it led to, provoked the latter into blocking that progress and returning to the earlier situation of imposed dependency. In the north-east of Brazil the *Ligas Camponeses* found their origin on an estate which demanded extravagant rents and tried to evict the peasants when they started to organize to buy the land. In the state of Veracruz in Mexico, it was the resistance of the landed elite to the execution of the agrarian reform law that provoked the peasants in the early twenties to build a militant organization.

The most strongly modernizing influence in Bolivia was undoubtedly the Chaco War, which took thousands of peasants from their more or less isolated villages into the army and gave them a view of other possibilities of life. The first leaders in Ucureña were ex-combatants. In Mexico the years of the armed struggle which was a part of the Revolution had a somewhat similar effect: the 'organizability' of the peasants was enhanced in many previously isolated areas which were touched by the struggle. Isolation and lack of perspective were broken in many regions of Mexico during the years of turmoil, so that the movements, once they were initiated, spread rapidly.

The experience of severe repression after a period of hope and initial change seems in both countries to have increased the willingness of the peasants to undertake drastic action to defend their interests: in Bolivia, the period of military regime between 1946 and 1952; and in Mexico, the restoration of the power of the military and old elite shortly after the success of the 1910 revolution.

Another characteristic that the regions where the movements described above took place have in common is their good accessibility and communication with urban centres. The state of Morelos is, at less than a hundred kilometres from Mexico City, an important supply area for that city. The Cochabamba valley where the Ucureña syndicate had its origin is closely linked to the town of Cochabamba and is one of the most productive agricultural regions of Bolivia. The Convención valley was undergoing a boom in coffee production and had good communications with the urban centre of Cuzco. In the areas in the north-east of Brazil where the *Ligas Camponeses* started, the influence of Recife is very important. An excellent road network links the rural areas with this city, and agriculture is comparatively highly developed. All these regions can be seen as relatively well-off compared with the national average. There was, however, acute frustration among the peasantry of those areas, and the regions were generally densely populated.

The peasants who participated in the initiation of the movements were not the poorest and most destitute. In the state of Morelos, the initiators of the movement were those who had been 'proletarianized' after having lived as independent small peasants belonging to *comunidades*. In the Cochabamba valley, the movement was initiated by landless peasants who aspired to become independent farmers, like some of their better-off neighbours, but who saw their efforts frustrated. The *arrendires* in La Convención were small farmers who saw the possibility of becoming independent; they were better off than most of the peasants living on estates in the Peruvian highlands. The peasants in the north-east of Brazil had experienced some improvement or were somewhat above the subsistence level. They all had relatively frequent urban contact of some kind.

Another important factor which these movements had in common was that their first leaders, although of peasant origin, had some kind of urban or modernizing (for example, travel) experience. Zapata was in the army and worked some time in Mexico City. José Rojas spent several years in Argentina and had some syndical organization experience in an urban environment before he became a peasant leader. In Morelos many peasants worked as wage-paid agricultural workers, a kind of rural 'proletariat', on the sugar plantations or in the mills. In the Cochabamba area a number of peasants had worked at some stage in their life in the mines, or had relatives working there. Also in La Convención and the north-east of Brazil, the initial leaders were migrants or had worked in urban centres. José dos Prazeres had many years' experience as a labour organizer and had participated in political movements. Among the leaders of the Federación Campesina of Venezuela there were many union organizers and even local merchants.

It generally appears that the peasants in many areas, in spite of considerable differentiation according to their relative well-being or their social status within the community, all have the same feeling of social distance regarding the large landowner, a uniting factor which generally seems to be stronger than inner divisions among them. There is indeed great differentiation within the peasantry, ranging from land-less rural proletariat to indigenous *comuneros*, but it seems that effective organization is possible among all these types once the condition of frustration or deprivation exists. The only groups that appear difficult to organize are the most destitute peasants who live at subsistence level, are highly dependent on their *patrón*, and live in isolated conditions or as migrant workers. It seems that such peasants join organized movements only when their lot becomes unbearable and for some reason an unorganized violent explosion results.

There appear to be some gradations in 'organizability'. From the various outstanding examples it appears that tenants or sharecroppers, who have a certain independence and manage their own plots, are relatively more apt to feel frustration and to take the initiative to organize than other types of landless peasants. Despoliation of land cultivated for many years without reimbursement for the improvements made, insecurity of tenure related to the arbitrary attitude of the landowners, and high rents often seem to be major causes for frustration. Many tenants have the feeling that the relatively large share of the produce or the cash which goes to the landowner is an unjustifiable expenditure. The more alert ones are well aware that the result of their toil is being conspicuously wasted in the cities in luxurious housing and other status-symbols. These views contribute to the feelings of frustration which the more independent and part-educated peasants have.

The present tendency in development policies in several countries, which apparently stress middle-class life-styles through conspicuous consumption, is a factor that tends to enhance the 'relative deprivation' and thus the 'organizability' of the majority of the peasants who stay on the periphery of these developments. The fact that in several countries the production or sale of luxury automobiles far exceeds that of tractors or small trucks is felt by peasant leaders to be relevant.

In addition to the modernizing influences and urban experience of the initial leaders, the areas where peasant movements began were influenced by what could be called 'rural promoters'. Although there were no community development programmes as such, there were certain modernizing agents working in the areas. Zapata received a great deal of help from the school teacher of his village, Otilio Montaño, and later from the lawyer Antonio Díaz Soto y Gama. The syndicate of Ucureña was strongly supported by the school teachers and was at one stage even led by the director of the school. The construction and maintenance of schools was in turn a main objective of the growing syndicates. This mutual collaboration was so effective that the local school system was chosen as a demonstration project by a community development agency. Also students and intellectuals of nearby Cochabamba gave support to the unions at various stages. It is not rare for some sons of landowners to align themselves, for personal or ideological reasons, with the peasantry against their own class: Arze Loureiro in Cochabamba and Julião in Pernambuco are cases in point.

The different movements were able to make a nationwide impact because of their alliance with a political movement at the national level which needed peasant support. Zapata's peasant guerrillas supported the new government of Madero in return for promises of agrarian reform. The Ucureña movement got a chance to develop fully and influence national policy after a revolutionary movement with which it had relations, and which was led by middle-class intellectuals and workers, had overthrown the old regime and dissolved the army. Since both national revolutionary movements were more or less middle-class oriented, continuous peasant pressure was needed in order to obtain the acceptance and the beginning of the implementation of an effective agrarian reform programme. This happened only after the peasants, through armed or non-violent occupation of estates in large territories, had shown that they were determined to struggle for their demands.

The peasant federation in Venezuela was almost completely organized by national and local political leaders of Acción Democrática. In the Convención valley there was considerable support from lawyers of the Communist labour unions of Cuzco and later from the Trotskyist movement mainly through the person of Hugo Blanco. In the state of Pernambuco in the north-east of Brazil the main urban supporters were politicians of one of the radical tendencies, including Julião, who was a socialist deputy.

These political allies had a radicalizing influence, but it seems that it was particularly the intransigence and violent reaction of the large landholders that acted as a stimulus to the radicalization of the peasant movements. The insistent and often violent opposition to demands such as the sale of lands for which too high rents were paid, the restitution of usurped lands or the acceptance of a proper land reform legislation provoked greater cohesiveness and drastic actions from these peasant groups. These actions at times went as far beyond orderly legal practices as did the activities of the landowners. One could almost say that the main opponents of peasant movements aided them by obliging them to unite and harness their forces.

It was clear in several cases that although a need for vengeance was strong among the peasants it was generally not expressed in destructive ways. In the Cochabamba area and La Convención as well as in the state of Morelos, the leaders saw to it that constructive measures were taken in addition to the elimination of the traditional system. Particularly in Bolivia, where the agrarian revolution was accompanied by little violence, some landlords who had not been abusive and had cultivated their lands well were respected and not subjected to the reform measures in the same way as their more abusive colleagues.

A great variety of tactics was used by landlords against the incipient movements. Intimidation, isolation, corruption or elimination of leaders or potential leaders of peasant movements appeared to be most frequent. Emiliano Zapata was drafted into the army even before his efforts to rally the peasants of his area became effective. After the movement had become strong and contributed to the Mexican Revolution, he was offered an estate for his services if he would give up further efforts to struggle for a real agrarian reform. Because he did not give in, he was assassinated in 1919. José Rojas in Bolivia was persecuted for several years, and after the 1952 Revolution the moderate leaders of the winning party, MNR, tried to sidetrack him by putting a less radical leader in his place; Rojas won a majority, however, among the peasants of the Cochabamba valley. Attempts were made to assassinate several leaders of the *Ligas Camponeses*, and some, such as João Pedro Teixeira of Sapé, fell in the struggle. In the Convención area, imprisonment, abusive treatment by the landlords and killings occurred. Many leaders of the Venezuelan FCV suffered persecution or exile in the years between 1948 and 1958, which made some of them martyrs. In all cases the effort to create representative peasant organizations could be undertaken only by persons willing to risk their lives.

After seeing some of the factors common to the few important peasant movements in Latin America as conditions favourable to their growth, some of the elements which played a role in the actual dynamics of this growth should be studied: (1) identification of an acutely felt need or grievance; (2) availability of leadership with some previous organizing experience, able to rally the peasants around this need or grievance; (3) the creation and consolidation of a following as a cohesive group around this leader; and (4) the alliance with urban supporters who link the organization with forces at the regional or national level.

## 2. AWARENESS OF GRIEVANCES AND FIRST STEPS

Most of the movements described here started with action from below and were formed because of an acutely felt need or grievance existing among the peasants. In the case of the Zapata movement the grievance resulted from the break-up of a more or less tolerable *status quo*. There was a strongly felt need to recover the lands which had been usurped and the independent status of peasants which had been lost. In the cases of Galileia in north-east Brazil, La Convención in Peru, as well as the Ucureña syndicate, the most strongly felt need that stimulated the peasants to unite and struggle was for the abolition of increasingly burdensome land tenure conditions; these were mainly the unpaid labour and services which had to be rendered to the landlord in exchange for a small plot of land, or an increasing rent which had to be paid.

The most acutely frustrating factor in these cases was

that when the peasants, strongly influenced by modernizing factors, hoped to improve their situation the landlords blocked this possibility and tried to maintain the old system more rigidly than before.

Once awareness of an acute problem existed the first steps to come to a solution were undertaken jointly. In practically all cases studied, the initial activities of the peasant groups strictly followed established and traditional legal channels to obtain the fulfilment of their needs. The village committee led by Emiliano Zapata as well as the peasant syndicate of Ucureña, the peasant league of Galileia and the unions of La Convención tried to defend their legitimate interests by appeals to the local courts or labour inspectors. However, the local courts and rural labour authorities in many Latin American countries were largely controlled or influenced by vested interests and decided only rarely in favour of the peasants. In the examples described in this book, the peasants soon learned that recourse to legal action gave no result and that power – primarily in the form of physical force – and not law is decisive in cases of conflicting interest. One CIDA report called this the 'lawlessness' which rules in most of rural Latin America.

That the peasantry has great respect for law and order is indicated by the fact that in all cases peasants initiated their activities with some form of legal action. In view of the poor results of peasant efforts in this respect one could even say that they have an exaggerated respect for the law and that they are overly 'legalistic'. The need to overcome the generally prevailing lawlessness can be seen as one of the most strongly felt needs of the peasants. The fact that governments are not able or willing to enforce the existing legislation in cases where it protects the peasants rather than the landlords is a strongly radicalizing stimulus in the rural areas. It is not surprising that among the demands expressed by peasants in the examples studied, in addition to the questions relating to a minimum of law and order and personal security (abolition of the most abusive and generally illegal practices of servitude), high importance was given to education. It is difficult to assess exactly what makes school education so attractive to the peasants, but it may well have important consequences for such elementary civil rights as the right to vote. In several Latin American countries the peasants are denied these rights as long as they are illiterate. Another basic civil right, more directly related to the formation of peasant organizations, that of freedom of association, is also denied to them in most countries.

In some countries, a willingness to apply legislation concerning freedom of association or labour protection seems to exist at the national level. But an effective enforcement apparatus at the local level exists only precariously. In some cases laws accepted at the national or federal level are not approved at the state level, or are applied at that level only after much delay and considerable weakening of the possible impact. There are many cases in the rural areas where the large landholders try – generally successfully – to impose their authority and power to circumvent national laws and international conventions, such as those of the ILO regarding freedom of association. It is not only in very isolated areas that the wealthy landowners effectively control or have a strong influence over the local authorities in charge of justice and the execution of the law. Even in countries where peasant organizations and their leaders are legally protected, strategies to hamper such organizations can easily be applied. It seems that a strong agitating or politicizing factor is not only the unwillingness of the landlords to make concessions but their opposition to peasant organization as such. In all the cases described here the intransigence of the rural power holders helped an initially moderate and timidly growing peasant organization to become conscious of the fact that there would be no solution of their problem, or survival of their organization, without a considerable change in the rural power structure.

The lack of basic civil rights and civil protection became immediately obvious after moderate efforts to achieve some improvements were initiated by the peasants. Opposition was of an intransigence and violence out of proportion to the moderation and 'legalistic' approach of the peasants. It was as if the landed elite felt that the whole *status quo* and all their privileges were at stake, once minor changes were allowed. In several of the cases described here the opposition of the landlords was directed not so much against the specific demands of the peasants, but against the fact that they made any demands at all or efforts to change their conditions. Even if one particular landowner was willing to give the peasants a chance of improvement, his neighbours or relatives, out of some kind of 'class solidarity', became alarmed, and violently blocked further progress, or reversed the trend. The cases of the Santa Clara estate in Ucureña and the *engenho* Galileia in Pernambuco are obvious examples. It is this type of opposition, then, that makes the peasants aware of the fact that they will not achieve even moderate improvements without changing the whole existing power structure.

The peasants' awareness of a need for overall change is expressed in some cases spontaneously in their adherence to messianic or millenarian movements created both by outsiders and by people from the peasantry. The difficulty is that, although peasants may see or feel the need for overall change, they do not clearly visualize ways and means through which this can be realized. It is at this crucial point that either peasants with urban experience, such as Zapata and José dos Prazeres, or urban leaders, such as Juan Guerra (the teacher in Ucureña) and Hugo Blanco, became important. They can channel the vague awareness of a need for change into a more concrete awareness of ways and means to change through organized effort.

It is obviously important to break through the isolation of the closed hacienda community in order that awareness of other possibilities can grow or be created among the peasantry. What occurred in Ucureña, Anenecuilco (Zapata's village) and La Convención with great difficulties and after much trial and error – a growth of awareness of the need and possibilities for change – can also be promoted through educational campaigns. The general grievances or needs of the peasants may not seem particularly acute at a certain moment but can become so through abusive acts by the landlords, and also through teaching or explaining.

The growth or creation among the peasants of an awareness of their basic needs and of the possibilities of demanding and struggling for the fulfilment of those needs has been called 'conscientization' in some countries, 'mobilization' or 'agitation' in others, and also 'politicization'. One case was the Basic Education Movement sponsored by the Church in the north-east of Brazil. The 'letters to peasants' published at times by Julião, or the orientation speeches given by Hugo Blanco and his helpers in La Convención, were other examples. The most important aspect of this process of creating awareness relates to the need to break through the impact of the traditional land tenure and power system, and the means through which this break may be accomplished.

One of the obstacles to the awareness of the need for radical change in cases where there are no blatant abuses is the fact that the traditional system has some more or less consciously applied defence mechanisms which prevent the peasants from seeing their situation clearly. Since the 'culture of repression' has prevailed for centuries certain elements have evolved in the system which soften its impact. This is the role of 'patronage'. Landlords, as long as they are solidly in control, try to maintain the image of being good fathers – in some cases they become godfathers to the children of their subjects. Such apparently benevolent 'patronage' relations can be created easily since the hacienda system is usually the only frame of reference for the peasants who grow up in it: they have no alternative. They are born into it, and there is practically no way of escaping from its impact. They are completely dependent on it for survival, and this dependency is strongly enforced. An additional difficulty is that the more able peasants often get special rewards, and are offered possibilities for individual improvement or have special ties to the landlord, so that they refrain from stimulating group action. Such people become foremen on the estates, rather than leaders of peasant interest groups.

It is clear that an important condition for the formation of a representative peasant organization is to break through the closedness, dependence and cohesion of the traditional 'patronage' system. This can generally be done only by the creation of new loyalties outside, and conflicting with, the traditional ones.

The stimulation of conflict to overcome the traditional influence of the landlord implies the promotion of awareness of the peasants' rational interests as contrary to the traditional bonds existing in the hacienda system. The cases described above, particularly the syndicate of Ucureña and the unions of La Convención, show that the fear and intransigence of the landed elite were a help in this respect. In fact, the lawlessness and the at times violent opposition of the landlords encountered by the peasants when they tried to form a representative organization within the traditional social climate practically forced them to greater internal cohesiveness. In the sociology of conflict, it is well known that it is easier to form a group when there is an opposing force than to form a group when there is no opposition. Thus the fact that the formation of representative peasant organizations is strongly opposed and creates a conflict situation may positively help to strengthen the cohesion of the new group.

In some of the more isolated areas where the 'culture of repression' of the hacienda system prevails almost undisturbed by modernizing influences, it seems that guerrilla groups can create an awareness among the peasants of the possibilities for change. This was at least the case with the group headed by Hector Béjar in some of the more isolated parts of the Ayacucho department of Peru in 1965. A small group of *guerrilleros* was able to win acceptance among the repressed peasants and become powerful and popular after an assault on the Chapi hacienda, whose owner had been particularly abusive. Several peasants joined the ranks of the small guerrilla group. The hacienda owners of the region began to fear, and several of them fled. Only considerable army and air force intervention made it possible to round up the group at the end of 1965. The military-civic action programme initiated in the region immediately after the defeat of the group brought the isolated communities and peasant groups under modernizing influences. Peasants seemed to be aware of the reasons that brought medical care and other modern facilities into their villages. They also realized that landlords were not as powerful as they had always appeared.

While in some respects peasant organizations in their formative stage can draw lessons from the syndical struggle of urban workers, it is important to note that there is considerable difference between a peasant movement and an urban labour organization involved in a conflict. While most industrial labour conflicts are solved in Latin America within the prevailing system, leaving the social structure of enterprises as such intact, solutions to the basic problems in rural areas can come about only through changes in the social structure. In labour conflicts there is often a basic consensus between employers and workers, which can be maintained in spite of a conflict over details such as the size of wages. Between the majority of the landlords and the peasantry, however, such consensus generally exists only if maintained by coercion. This is a basic fact which must be taken into account.

In this respect also the question of whether or not the struggle should be directed towards economic or political goals becomes important. The examples of more or less successful peasant movements described coincide in stressing some kind of political struggle. Struggle for such concrete objectives as the return of usurped lands (the Zapata movement) or the liberation from servitude of small peasants through the buying or renting of land (the movements in Ucureña and La Convención) encountered so much opposition from the local power elite that the struggle automatically became political. This appears to be the main characteristic of the agrarian struggle in Latin America to date, and it would be unreasonable not to focus peasant organization activities accordingly.

An important aspect of the new groups, however, is the services they render, where possible, to the peasants. Some of the Peasant Leagues in Brazil founded centres where medical assistance was given to members. The unions in La Convención did a great deal to foster education and agricultural extension, anti-drinking habits and certain aspects of home economics such as the use of beds and shoes. It was noted in Chaupimayo that, long after Hugo Blanco was jailed, peasants continued to wear beards (as their leader did) and shoes, in distinction to the areas farther away where the daily impact of the educational effort had been less. Such service or activities are a means of guaranteeing the loyalty of members during periods of calm in the struggle to solve more basic issues.

Among peasant and labour union leaders a problem often discussed is how to gain enough concrete benefits to keep members interested and militant, and at the same time to keep the struggle for overall social change awake. Members sometimes tend to be content with minor adjustments and gains, and forget about the basic social change needed to bring them a real and enduring improvement, such as redistribution of land. In La Convención as well as the north-east of Brazil, this problem came up. There were those who wanted to follow the more radical line (those who voted for Hugo Blanco to head the La Convención peasant federation), while the more moderate peasants preferred the older and less radical leaders. The *Ligas Camponeses* organized a good number of services for their members and gained direct benefits, but they always emphasized the importance of the final purpose, agrarian reform rather than piecemeal improvement. It seems, particularly where the basic needs of the peasants cannot be solved without radical changes in the rural social structure, that it is best to begin the struggle, and gain strength, through winning concrete minor changes: better tenancy rates, prevention of eviction, abolition of servitude conditions, and so on. To win one case against a landlord is an encouraging experience, and the next steps will be easier to take. Opposition of the landlords to even minor changes, which merely imply the execution of existing laws (regarding wages or tenancy, for example), enhances the will to struggle among the peasants once they see that this struggle is not completely hopeless. Small successes are essential for this process.

## 3. THE ROLE OF LEADERSHIP

A most important factor in the formative stage of a peasant organization is the quality of the leadership. As shown already, a primary objective in the formation of new organizations is to achieve independence from the traditional *patrón*. This can take place when peasants become 'followers' of a leader, with whom the relationship of dependency is less unilateral and monopolistic than with the hacienda *patrón*. A peasant leader is as dependent on the support of the members as the members are dependent on his leadership. Such groups initially take the form of a 'following' around an inspiring and strong personality, a local peasant. A feeling of togetherness grows at the same time as the feeling in favour of supporting and following the respected and exemplary leader. The important point is that this 'following' of a peasant leader has to grow in competition or even conflict with the already existing ties of the hacienda system.

This was to a large extent the case at the time the Peasant Leagues were started in Brazil. The approach of José dos Prazeres, their initiator, as well as of Francisco Julião, who later became the more or less charismatic leader of the Leagues, was rather paternalistic. It should be noted, however, that this form of protective and independence-stimulating paternalism was the approach the peasants of the northeast best understood and which appealed to them. This type of paternalism, and the 'patronage' element belonging to it, is not aimed at maintaining itself, but tries rather to provoke increasing initiative and independence among the members of a group. The leaders of this new 'following' purposely tried to create a social group climate with democratic or participatory tendencies, respecting the peasants and their opinions and defending their interests.

Francisco Julião, himself the son of a local landowner, used his and his brother's estates to hold the meetings of the Leagues, which were forbidden and persecuted on the surrounding estates. He purposely stimulated the associational capacity of the peasants. Hugo Blanco went much farther in his identification with the peasants: he became a peasant himself. The farm where he lived became a training centre for the whole Convención area. Peasants usually seem to need a leader who through his personality gives them a sense of strength and discipline and courage to overcome great odds. The personal example set by such a leader has to represent these characteristics in an abundant way. This was apparently the case with Zapata, José Rojas, José dos Prazeres, Julião, Hugo Blanco and others.

These cases seem to confirm the view that peasants often (but not always) tend to see as an ideal political leader an imposing, masculine (*macho*) personality sufficiently strong to be able to overcome their fear of organizing and of getting involved in risky organizational efforts. Practically all organizations and movements have, in their initial stage, a leader with charismatic qualities, who knows how to inspire people and bring them to united action. Sometimes this implies the ability to be violent and aggressive so as to trigger off political action in spite of strong opposition.

It is characteristic of charismatic leaders that they themselves create or tolerate the creation of a myth around their personality. They accept certain postures or terminology impressive to peasants. This becomes clear from Julião's statements and letters to peasants, and from the fact that José Rojas refused to speak any language other than Quechua. Such 'messianistic' elements may be helpful in the initial stage, but at a later stage, when the movement begins to develop and is gaining strength, they may become counterproductive.

A great deal depends on the qualities of the new leader as a *patrón* of his group. He can become a dominating personality on whom the followers depend, and his domination of his 'following' can become almost as coercive as that of the traditional hacienda system. Particularly in the stage where the struggle of the organization is difficult, and the leader depends on the willingness of his followers to participate actively and back him up, chances for such developments are relatively small. Then active support, sometimes the risking of lives, of the members is needed.

Once the new group is strong enough to be a real challenge to the traditional system, efforts will be undertaken by the traditional system to neutralize its impact. This is particularly the case where the new group tends to be directed not only towards some concrete benefits for its members but towards a radical change in the rural social structure and the elimination of the landlords as a class.

In view of the need to compete or conflict with hacienda 'patronage', it seems that the most suitable for leading their peers in the agrarian struggle are those persons with leadership qualities who have gone out of the villages and returned with modern insights and new skills. An increasing number of actual and potential peasant leaders have had experience of urban life. Many initiators and leaders have had the experience while doing compulsory military service, the most striking example being Emiliano Zapata. Others have worked in the towns or in the mines, or as migrant workers in highly developed areas. In Bolivia, Peru and Chile, the influence of peasants who became miners and later went back to their villages has been important. It should be noted that the difference between miners and peasants is frequently vague, since many miners are recruited from peasant families and return to agriculture when silicosis or some other illness makes further work in the mines too dangerous for them.

In some of the more isolated communities a person who is literate, and has thus learned how to deal with the outside world, can become an outstanding leader, surpassing in importance the traditional leaders.

An outstanding factor, important in past and present cases, is the personal quality of the leader. Incorruptibility, in the face of the manipulations of the opposing interests, is highly important. It seems that the personal qualities of leaders are often related to or influenced by their ideological orientation. Many of those who are outstanding because of their personal qualities belong to religious or ideological groups that emphasize honesty, exemplary personal behaviour, zeal and diligence, self-discipline, a great sense of justice and other characteristics crucial for good leadership. Thus leaders are sometimes militant Protestants, Communists, or socialists or inspired by the Social-Christian tendencies renovating Catholicism in some countries. Among the outstanding leaders in the La Convención area of Peru were Protestants whose exemplary behaviour impressed their neighbours. In the Brazilian north-east, several outstanding leaders were members or ex-members of the Communist Party, while others were devout Catholics. Although belonging to a specific religion or ideology that requires a certain behaviour and discipline from its adherents is not a prerequisite for being an exemplary leader, there is a frequent coincidence.

Naturally, personal characteristics can be a risk as well as an asset for successful peasant organization. A great deal depends on the social system in which the leaders are functioning. This overall system is usually not a guarantee that the best qualities of peasant leaders are stimulated, nor that the best natural leaders necessarily rise to the surface. On the contrary, one serious problem faced by peasant organizations is the tendency of leaders to utilize the organization to further their own ambitions. Leaders do become co-opted by the power elite of the countryside, which is rarely favourable to effective peasant organization. In the process they tend to cease defending the interests of the peasants. This could be called political corruption. Economic corruption is another temptation: the misuse of the resources of the organization or the acceptance of bribes. Another problem is that personal rivalry between leaders over power or economic gains may lead to internal struggles. Internal division may also arise from ideological rivalry. Such rivalries are often related to or stimulated by outside forces of some kind.

## 4. URBAN SUPPORT AND REGIONAL ORGANIZATION

The leaders of the peasant organizations described have complemented their ability to rally people against an abusive landowner with the ability to build up and direct a broader organization. Several local peasant communities were brought together not only to face one particular landowner, but the hacienda system as such, as it functioned in a whole area.

From the experiences described here, it is clear that the formation of new groups at the community level, important as it may be, is not enough to break through the traditional system. The Vicos experiment in Peru indicated that one traditional hacienda can be transformed into a democratically-led community without having much influence on the traditional system as a whole. Isolated pilot experiments, where considerable improvements in the life of the peasants have been made, have existed in many countries, but their only effect lies in some degree of awakening the surrounding peasants to their potential – an increase in 'organizability' as a result of frustration. This may not lead directly to the effective formation of similar groups and the extension of the pilot experience to a large area.

It is at this critical stage that contact with urban sympathizers who are willing to be allies in the struggle against the traditional and vested rural interests becomes highly important. The linkage of local peasant organizations with a wider framework of mutual or outside support, or a combination of both, comes out in all examples as a crucial factor in the success of new groups.

Zapata's movement began at the village level and initially integrated only a few communities. It gained momentum when it joined in the overall revolutionary struggle and then found several sympathizers, such as the local school teacher and later the lawyer and politician Díaz Soto y Gama, in the building-up of an effective regional organization with some kind of legal basis (the Plan de Ayala). The syndicate of Ucureña was supported as it began to be established and spread through the area by school teachers and former miners. Later, the growing movement was related to political parties working at the national level, such as the PIR and MNR. The Peasant Leagues in the Brazilian north-east were supported by lawyers and other professionals, who gave the organization a region-wide structure. The Leagues were specially designed as a centralized body with nuclei in many places in order to increase their effectiveness. The unions of La Convención became influential after forming a federation. They were then able to apply for help from urban lawyers and politicians, who helped to create a regional structure. The need for any local peasant organization to join with other similar groups and to form a federation of some kind is a *sine qua non* for gaining influence.

An important advantage of federation of local unions, or other community or peasant organizations, is that it is a definitive step in the breaking-up of the traditional social system dominated by the hacienda. The peasants become aware that in other communities in neighbouring areas people have similar problems to their own. This psychological factor may help to overcome any initial fear of resisting or breaking with the local social system.

The importance of forming federations of community organizations cannot be stressed enough. Another of its psychological effects is the feeling of power which people get when belonging to a large-scale regional movement. It has been observed in many instances, such as at the First Congress of Peasants of Pernambuco, Brazil, and the Indian Congress in La Paz, Bolivia, in 1945, that peasants for the first time in their life get a feeling of power and importance when they have a regional meeting, and march by the hundreds through the streets of an important city to represent their interests and show themselves as a unified body. Mass meetings and parades of this type have an important function during the formation process of a peasant organization: to strengthen the self-esteem of the peasantry and to impress public opinion. Such occurrences help the peasants overcome the effects of having lived for centuries in the 'culture of repression'.

In this respect, it can be seen how important it is to have a regional headquarters, which serves as an office and meeting place for the growing organization. Such physical amenities give the organization an identity. The name is written on a plate at the entrance, and any peasant coming to the main city of his region can always find peers and comrades from different places representing the same interests. For those who have been living dependent on one man, the *patrón*, with the hacienda as their only point of reference, this is an important means of widening perspective.

Once a local group sees the need for joining a federation with other groups in similar conditions, the more or less charismatic peasant leader(s) who started the movement can be overshadowed by more sophisticated charismatic leaders or politicians. To some extent this happened in Ucureña, Bolivia, when José Rojas took the leadership; it occurred very clearly in the Peasant Leagues of the Brazilian northeast where Julião became increasingly important and in the peasant federation of La Convención where Hugo Blanco took over. In the movement directed by Zapata in Morelos, Mexico, the initial charismatic leader kept his position throughout the time the movement was extending its influence.

In order to prevent the cohesion and strength of a large group becoming dependent on one strong leader, and to guarantee the effective participation of its members, it is

essential for the charismatic leadership – the initially mobilizing factor in a movement – to become institutionalized. The
membership starts to feel increasingly that it belongs to an
organized and structured movement, or to a party with a
more or less defined ideology, representing their needs. This
process was initiated in the Peasant Leagues of Brazil but was
well on its way in the movement in La Convención, Peru.
In Brazil, the Leagues had, just before they were destroyed
in April 1964, started a campaign to create a 'political organization' of a 'Leninist' type within the local branches, to give
cohesion and a more defined structure to the whole movement.

In Bolivia, the process of structuring the movement took
place after the peasant federation in the area where it origin-
ated, Cochabamba, had shown its power. National political
leaders, particularly Paz Estenssoro, used the Movimiento
Nacionalista Revolucionario party to spread the peasant
movement into the whole country and to institutionalize it
into a national framework, related to MNR interests.

The Venezuelan peasant federation was created and built
up as a nationwide political structure from the outset, although officially the Federation was founded after local
unions and state *seccionales* had been organized by activists
of the Acción Democrática party.

While support from national political and ideological
groups can be an asset and help to spread or strengthen a
peasant organization, it can also be a source of weakness.
Through the alliance with national movements over which
they have no control, the peasants can become involved in
the political and ideological rivalries existing at that level.
This was clear in the Venezuelan FCV, which purged the
relatively radical original leadership in order to bring federation policies into line with the overall national policies of
Acción Democrática, which was becoming increasingly iden-

tified with the middle class. Similarly the Mexican CNC was transformed into a political clientele of the official middle-class dominated party to control the peasant vote rather than to defend peasant interests.

In the Peasant Leagues in the north-east of Brazil and in the Peasant Federation of La Convención, rivalries among the leaders produced divisions or confusion at the grass roots. Several pamphlets and periodicals show these internal divisions. This was in part a result of ideological differences between leaders over strategy. In the Convención movement, one faction wanted to use a less radical approach than that advocated by Hugo Blanco. In the *Ligas Camponeses* the division concerned the structure of the movement. For years the Leagues expressed themselves mainly through agitation, while some groups internally advocated a tighter political organization, apparently against the wishes of Julião. These divisions were not only along ideological lines but also a result of personal rivalries. When political groups in power in Pernambuco or in the country as a whole needed the electoral support of the Leagues, political ambitions became a dividing issue between some of the top leaders.

Particularly important for the success of peasant organizations are the kinds of demands they and their leaders bring forward. While most of the movements described or mentioned in this book started by demanding moderate changes and improvements, the opposition of the landlords stimulated radicalization or escalation of the demands. Radical change in the overall power and land tenure became the main focus of the peasants' struggle in all cases. In the escalation of their demands the urban supporters of the peasants gave considerable guidance. It seems that the movements derived part of their cohesion and strength from the overwhelming importance of the demand for land, rather than from minor benefits. Peasant organizations which focused only on wage increases or similar adjustments in the *status quo* were more liable to decay or were outstripped by more radical organizations.

It seems that clearcut, radical demands for land distribution or restitution, and leadership which in a rather uncompromising way leads the peasants in the struggle for these demands, ensure a strong cohesion in the organization and active participation of the peasants. The movements led by Zapata in Mexico, Hugo Blanco in La Convención, José Rojas in Ucureña, and the 1958–60 period of the FCV in Venezuela are cases in point. Simple slogans such as 'Land and Freedom' (*'Tierra y Libertad'*) or 'Land or Death' (*'Tierra o Muerte'*) rallied peasants into large-scale organized activities. This is no guarantee, however, that effective political peasant participation will continue once this main demand has been fulfilled, or is in the course of being fulfilled. The problem which can result will be discussed in the next section, which shows how peasant organizations which flourished during the height of the struggle for land reform could soon after success be partly or wholly neutralized.

## 5. THE DEMAND FOR LAND AND APPROPRIATE MEANS OF STRUGGLE: A PROCESS OF ESCALATION

As is evident from almost all examples and cases known in Latin America, the political role of peasant organizations in the struggle for land has generally not been very orderly. It has often taken a spontaneous and at times a violent form. In some countries only after agrarian reform was well under way could peasant participation be channelled through newly created institutions, such as trades unions or political organizations. This is a direct result of the situation described in the first chapter: the lawlessness and 'culture of repression' prevailing in the rural areas and the severe obstacles created by the opposition of traditional vested interests to orderly and institutionalized but dynamic reform of the land tenure structure.

The resistance to change of the landed elite, and its influence in the national governments, directly or indirectly provoked the drastic, even violent forms which the peasants' actions have taken, often with guidance or leadership from urban groups. This is most obvious from the case of Mexico, where the first agrarian legislation (of 1915) was a result of a strong peasant reaction to evictions and abuses, which was expressed in a violent revolutionary movement. Later this legislation could be applied only because of the determined resistance of the peasantry in various regions to the violent measures taken by landowners to block its application. The Bolivian reform would have been inconceivable without the strongly organized pressure of the peasants in the Cochabamba area. In Venezuela, pressure by the Federación Campesina de Venezuela, particularly the many peaceful land invasions after the fall of the Pérez Jiménez regime in 1958, was crucial to agrarian reform.

In those countries which have hesitantly initiated agrarian reform the same 'explosive forces' are at work as operated in the countries which already have an effective programme. It will be important to know what kind of disorder or unrest is unavoidable and how the different forces can be most effectively used. In this respect it is particularly important to discuss the forms of direct action by peasants through which agrarian reform legislation and its implementation have been achieved or accelerated. Various forms of direct action have been employed by peasant groups after encountering insurmountable obstacles in presenting their demands through the normal legal channels. When dealing with the radical action methods used by peasants, it cannot be stressed enough that in all the examples studied here these means were used only after the legal and institutionalized channels of problem solution had been consistently blocked because of intransigent landlord opposition.

Among the forms of direct pressure which peasants have exercised are sit-down strikes and the occupation of unused lands and of those lands which the peasants petitioned for or which were in dispute. These activities, or even more drastic ones such as armed revolt, were the only ways open to the peasants to pressure for reform. The cases described show overwhelmingly that practically all agrarian reform activity in Latin America has, until today, been the direct or indirect result of such activities.

In some cases, such as Mexico in the Cárdenas period, Bolivia after 1952 and Venezuela after 1958, these organizational activities were supported, stimulated or tolerated by the government and/or the political party in power, in spite of the fact that a certain amount of chaos sometimes resulted from this policy. This happened in Bolivia in 1952–3, and was related to the fact that the reform efforts started there after six years of severe repression (1946–52). A return to that situation was threatening as the landlords attempted to overthrow the reformist government. Direct action of peasants was also organized in Venezuela in 1958–60 – under somewhat similar conditions after ten years of repression (1948–58). The land invasions, though ostensibly disapproved of, were tacitly tolerated by the authorities; as the reform process got under way they could be channelled and directed.

A careful study of the various forms of direct action taken by peasants to bring across their demands for agrarian reform measures points to some important factors. Most cases show a process of escalating demands. Land reform as such often becomes an issue after other, less drastic, demands have met with intransigence on the part of the landed elite. The escalation of demands is generally accompanied by an escalation of the means used to press for these demands. Initial demands often include the abolition of practices which interfere with basic – and often constitutionally established – civil rights, such as personal freedom. Others concern the recognition of traditional property rights, security of tenure or compensation for improvements made if the tenancy of a certain plot has had to be given up. Most have a firm legal basis, but the law is, at the local and at times at the national level, either ignored or interpreted in favour of the landlords, who have the power.

The peasants appear to be too legalistic in their approach. Initially, the means used to present demands are moderate: petitions, lawsuits, and complaints to the labour inspector. Since relief through these legally established channels is generally not obtained, wherever peasants have some organizing experience or can count on support from people with such experience, other means are tried; but this only comes after the legal approach has proved fruitless. Examples are: the years of legal struggle of the peasant communities headed by Zapata before they joined the Revolution; the legal arrangements achieved by the first peasant union in Ucureña in Bolivia in 1936, undone by the landlords in 1939; the year-long struggle in the court of Recife by the first Brazilian Peasant League, to avoid the illegal dislodgement of peasants from plots that they had occupied for years. These are all cases that testify to the peasants' respect for legal and orderly means. To have existing laws respected, rather than over-ruled by intransigent landlords, is often the basic issue around which peasants start to become active. Whether a growing peasant organization initiates its activities with a struggle for civil rights against illegal practices of the landlords, or for economic improvements, or for agrarian reform, depends on the local situation. To start with the issues which have the best chances of successful solution seems sound strategy in the period when the leaders and followers of an organization are gaining self-confidence.

The escalation of demands and of the means used to pressure for them appears generally to have been a reaction to the uncompromising attitude of the landlords. If moderate demands and forms of pressure are completely ignored or even ridiculed by those in power, more radical forms are tried. More recently, having learned from past experiences, peasant organizations have begun to use the escalation of demands as a conscious strategy to achieve significant social reforms.

Although not always openly expressed, agrarian reform has been among the main objectives of most peasant movements from their beginning. In some cases this idea came up among the more alert peasant leaders – usually where peasants had been despoiled of their ancestral lands. In other cases the idea of radical reform was introduced by urban leaders and supporters of a peasant movement, such as Hugo Blanco in Peru or Francisco Julião in Brazil. Seeing that a radical agrarian reform was the only solution for the existing rural inequities, but that the majority of the peasants had not yet realized it, these leaders tried to create an awareness of this need; this was done not only through *concientización*, teaching and explaining the social implications of rural underdevelopment, but also through the struggle itself. By showing, time after time, that the landlords would not grant moderate, legally guaranteed demands and civil rights, it was easily demonstrated to the peasants that only radical changes in the rural power structure could lead to fulfilment of their demands and redress of their grievances.

This escalation of awareness through the struggle for civil rights and other basic needs has in some cases had considerable success. It has the additional advantage that the peasants learn gradually to overcome their traditional fear of opposing the rural elite; they start facing this opposition on issues where justice and common sense are so overwhelmingly on their side that they feel they can take the risk. These are also issues where the attitude of the landlords is flagrantly in conflict with law and order. The landlords' refusal to give in to legitimate demands diminishes their traditional prestige in the eyes of their workers, and of public opinion.

In many areas peasants had never contemplated the possibility of using means more radical than a petition or an appeal to justice. Radical means had not been tried consistently, and their uselessness was accepted almost as a fact of life. Once it was demonstrated that following through on a case with dedicated legal help made the landlords uneasy and intransigent, the use of more radical means appeared to be feasible.

One of the means which in most countries falls well within the established legal framework is the strike. This usually consists of a refusal to work at critical moments of the agricultural cycle after all demands have been bluntly refused. Where the peasants have become acquainted with the labour struggle, such as in areas of Peru and Bolivia where peasants work during certain periods of their life in the mines, peasant organizations have noted the uses made by labour organizations of the legitimate forms of struggle.

An important type of peasant strike is to refuse to provide free labour services to the landlord – obligations which are today outlawed, but not eradicated in most countries. In Bolivia between 1939 and 1952, the peasants frequently went on sit-down strikes (*huelgas de brazos caídos*) against the landowners for varying lengths of time, sometimes for years. This non-violent means of action contrasted with the spontaneous and violent outbursts of protest that had frequently occurred before in Bolivia. The large number of complaints made by the landowners in the press and to the authorities about these strikes indicated their effectiveness.

It seems that the 'violence potential' of the peasants' direct action method is far less important than it is in the labour movement. There is no danger of damage to anyone's goods or life involved, as there is in a street demonstration, where shopkeepers or the city traffic can suffer damage. In the peasants' sit-down strike the disadvantages are not on the side of the peasants but rather of their opponents: the peasants have more time to work their subsistence plot.

A form of action used by the peasants more frequently than the sit-down strike is the peaceful occupation or 'invasion' of unused or underused lands belonging to large estates. Many of the agrarian reform efforts carried out in Latin America are a direct or indirect result of such activities. However, a great deal of misunderstanding exists about this approach, which is often branded as 'violence'. It is, however, a mistake to consider peasant 'invasions' as acts of violence. On the contrary, most acts of violence related to the agrarian reform issue have come from the landlords, and violent action by the peasants has generally come only as a reaction to this. The peasant guerrillas of Zapata, the rural defence units organized among the peasants by President Cárdenas in the late thirties in Mexico, the forceful take-over of estates, and the driving-out of the most abusive landlords in the initial stage of the agrarian revolution in Bolivia were all reactions against landlord violence.

On the other hand, most occupations of unused lands have been of a non-violent and at times explicitly peaceful nature. In cases where peasants occupied privately owned but unused land, the action could often be interpreted as a form of 'civil disobedience', an accepted form of non-violent pressure.

When considering the invasions as an appropriate means of struggle for the peasants the problem of legitimacy of landed property should be mentioned. The CIDA study on Peru indicated that by 'invasions' was understood the actual occupation by dispossessed peasants of land in the hands of the haciendas. The report noted that the peasants did not see such 'invasions' as illegitimate, because they considered them to be the recovery of lands which had been taken away from them illegally. Many of the lands occupied had been for years in litigation, but were occupied by the large landholders in the meantime and often very extensively used, while peasants lived on surrounding, overcrowded mountain slopes. It seems that the invasions were in many cases an expression of the peasants' attachment to legality rather than a desire to subvert the existing order. In many cases in Peru peasants reasoned that the manner in which their traditional claims were honoured benefited only the large landholder in forms which they considered illegitimate.

From the peasants' point of view there appears to be a sound logic in the occupation and bringing into effective use of idle or underused lands. This is particularly so if they have been illegally despoiled, as has happened in many cases. It seems that in most cases where invasions have taken place they were rather a constructive non-violent reaction to such violence as despoliation and efforts to assassinate leaders. Rather than taking vengeance on the landlord or destroying his goods, the peasants occupied unused or underused lands and brought them under cultivation.

In most countries, even if the lack of 'social function' of private lands was recognized as a problem, occupation of such land by peasants was officially condemned. In Venezuela the government officially took up its position against the invasions of estates which were not efficiently cultivated or which had been alienated from the peasants by illegal means, yet the invasions were encouraged by the peasants' unions belonging to the government party. Most of the invaded estates in Venezuela were later purchased from the landlords and distributed among the peasants under the agrarian reform programme. In Peru, where the return of formerly usurped land and the distribution of estate land was promised to the peasants during election campaigns, a special clause was included in the 1964 agrarian reform law indicating that lands which had been invaded would not be considered for official land distribution. In fact, however, invasions were initially tolerated and several invaded estates were distributed among the peasants.

How seriously the legitimacy of private land property is taken by the peasants depends a great deal on how seriously it is taken by those who have the power to interpret and execute the laws.

The problem of the legitimacy of landed property should be seen in its historical context. Traditional titles continue to be respected by indigenous peasants in spite of their hopeless efforts to get them honoured in the courts. Many *comunidades* in Latin America keep title documents that date from the colonial epoch. In Guatemala, in several municipalities with a predominantly indigenous population, the Indians conserve with care and ceremony the municipal titles which they inherited from their forefathers. These officially invalid titles are more recognized by the peasants than the titles of private property that have been issued, one way or another, since the end of the last century.

In the case of land invasions where property rights are in dispute, or where the law or the constitution does not protect privately owned lands which do not fulfil their 'social function', occupations by peasants cannot be seen as acts of disobedience. In spite of this, in many countries the press, often influenced by the landlords, denounces such activities as 'violence' or 'violations of the law'. On occasions where such acts take place, violence can sometimes occur because alarming publicity stimulates police or army intervention to be more drastic than necessary under the circumstances.

However, when idle lands are peacefully occupied by landless peasants and are brought under cultivation, there is no question of violence. On the other hand, the eviction of squatters from formerly unused lands which they have cleared and cultivated for years, or the dislodging of peasants by burning their houses, is clearly an act of violence, often supported by the authorities.

It is obvious from almost all the cases of successful peasant movements that violence, that is the intentional destruction of life or property, has been used by only a few of them. Except for the Mexican Revolution (the Zapata movement and other peasant struggles related to that event) and the initial stages of the Bolivian agrarian revolution, most of the violence in the agrarian struggles has come from the landlords. The proverbial attachment of the peasant to security, order and lawfulness explains why there have not been more acts of vengeance and violence than those that have sporadically occurred. This seems surprising in the light of the fact that the peasantry in many parts of Latin America live permanently in a state of lawlessness, 'culture of repression', institutionalized violence and abusiveness of the landlords.

It appears from most known cases that where the peasants are given institutionalized opportunities to bring about a radical change in the rural power structure these opportunities are used with moderation and with respect for those who are to lose their privileged position, rather than with a desire for vengeance. The best example is the Bolivian agrarian reform, which was the most drastic. Although in the preliminary struggle, over many years, numbers of peasant leaders had been assassinated, once the power relationships had changed, the lives and, in most instances, the personal property of the landlords were respected. Only where the landlords themselves engaged in violent opposition were their lives endangered. No cases are known (but some cases probably did occur) where landlords were persecuted for their former abuses or crimes after the power relationships had changed. Usually the peasants felt that to have been given land was enough. In the most radicalized areas, they merely refused to let the abusive landlords return to their former estates. In some of these cases peasant leaders visited the former landlords in their town houses in order to make deals or arrangements related to the transfer of land.

Some landlords even received payments or contributions from their former subjects without this being necessary under the law. There was no call for 'popular justice' or anything similar, although landlords in some areas feared this. This fear was, however, probably more a result of the landlords' 'bad conscience' than of their understanding of the peasants.

It seems that the violent resistance of the landlords to moderate peasant demands is related to their irrational fear of the peasants' vengeance once free of their bondage. The saying about not giving a finger because then they take the whole hand is in many cases a conscious and openly expressed element in the approach of the rural elite.

In comparisons of the various movements in which strikes or land occupations of some kind had an important role, it is apparent that most of them were limited to specific geographic regions. The most successful movements did not take place spontaneously in one community, but rather were carried out in a coordinated way in a whole region, such as the upper Cochabamba valley in Bolivia, the Convención valley in Peru, the state of Morelos in Mexico; also some of the densely populated states of Venezuela. In some of those regions the movements were more intense, and more successful, than in others, but generally they had a sufficient geographic concentration to give the peasants the feeling that their region was on the move, and that their efforts were not just scattered and uncoordinated protest actions. This explains the relative success in most of these regions of such efforts as were made to mobilize the peasants for development after land reform had been carried out. Specifically, in some areas of Mexico in the Cárdenas period and in the Convención valley this was the case. But as a rule peasant mobilization was not utilized to bring about a really sustained regional development.

On the whole it seems that the means used by the peasants were usually such that, with a minimum of extra legality, a maximum of concrete benefits or security could be achieved, mainly the possession of the land which they tilled. As soon as the peasants' demands were satisfied, and the land they worked was in their possession, in most cases they lost interest in the political movement as a whole. Hugo Blanco declared on various occasions after his movement had been calmed through military action and land distribution that he was disappointed in the revolutionary spirit of the peasants. The peasants of the Galileia estate in Pernambuco, Brazil, are another case in point. It seems, however, that the landlords have so much fear of change that they take a stand which provokes the peasantry to use increasingly radical means. Thus the peasant movement became in some cases a revolutionary factor in the society as a whole, in spite of the originally limited demands and the moderate attitude of the peasants. In those areas where the peasants took to radical forms of action, their civil violence occurred generally as a direct response to landlord intransigence and violence, and because no other ways were open to them.

# CHAPTER 7

# The Political Implications:
# An Increasing Revolutionary
# Potential?

The whole issue of escalation of peasant demands as a reaction to landlord intransigence clearly demonstrates that peasants are not revolutionaries by birth, but neither are they any longer the passive victims of traditional or modern forms of domination. They let themselves be repressed, exploited and utilized, but the resulting frustration brings an increasing awareness that other ways are open to them. In the present chapter an effort will be made to show that the 'culture of repression' in Latin America is becoming increasingly felt by the peasants as illegitimate.

Peasants have had a variety of experiences that have promoted awareness of possibilities for change.

1. In some cases, peasant groups that have tried to overcome the effects of acute frustration have not been allowed to spread or have been repressed (in the Convención valley in Peru and the north-east of Brazil). It seems that in such cases conditions for more radical movements are being created.

2. Elsewhere movements growing from below have gained sufficient power to achieve important benefits and an institutionalized role on the national political scene. This happened in Mexico and Bolivia (after 1952), but, particularly in Mexico, the influence of the organized peasantry was later neutralized by co-option and integration in a dominating political system. Only in Cuba, it seems, has the peasantry

achieved or been given an active share in the national development effort and its benefits.

3. In some countries, more or less 'populist' or reform-oriented governments have at times made their appearance and have contributed to an awakening of the peasants. The latter were allowed or even stimulated to organize from above, as happened in Venezuela, Guatemala (before 1954) and Brazil (1963–4), but as soon as the possibility for effective change grew these 'populist' governments were overthrown by conservative forces. This was possible because there was no strongly organized peasantry to defend the government. The period of repression that followed in these cases seems, however, to be a main condition for a radicalization of the peasants, who will probably come into action at a later stage more strongly than ever (as occurred in Venezuela in 1958 after the repressive military government was overthrown). The various ways in which the peasantry of Latin America experience frustration may well make them increasingly willing to participate in radical or revolutionary movements, as has happened in some past cases. Whether this revolutionary potential will be utilized depends on the extent to which urban allies will be prepared to support and guide such movements effectively.

## 1. THE 'CULTURE OF REPRESSION' AND ILLEGITIMACY

At present even peasants in remote areas get some idea of political forces at the national level through the modern means of mass communication. This factor counted for little in the past, when only such events as the Chaco War (Bolivia, 1933–6) or '*la violencia*' (Colombia, 1948–58) shook up peasant society sufficiently to create awareness regarding national political forces and conflicts. In areas where repression has been severe and where not only the local government and police, but also the national government through the army, has taken a position against the peasants, awareness sometimes takes the form of resentment, if not hatred. It is precisely in such countries as El Salvador, where repression has been extremely severe (the genocide of between 20,000 and 30,000 people in the early thirties), that a constant semi-military control over the rural areas has to be maintained in order to prevent the hatred from becoming overt aggression.

In areas where repression is less acute and obvious, more subtle forms of the 'culture of repression' are increasingly felt as such. Peasants learn about elections and popular participation, but serious doubts and distrust remain. Most regimes seem to be distrusted because they are repressive.

When a regime felt as repressive, and thus illegitimate, breaks down, the peasants easily seem to take the law into their own hands and give up their, on the whole, overly legalistic attitude. Once the 'lid is off', the peasants defend their interests by means that cannot be controlled even by their own leaders. This happened to a large extent in Bolivia after the years of repression during 1946–52, and in Venezuela to some extent after 1958, when the repressive climate suddenly disappeared for reasons which were not directly influenced by the peasants. In such cases those peasants who had in earlier periods enjoyed some improvement or had justified expectations were the first to take action, not those who had always been repressed in a more or less constant way under the traditional system. The relatively more prosperous and developing areas of Cochabamba in Bolivia and the states of Aragua and Carabobo in Venezuela became the scenes of spontaneous radical peasant action.

The success or failure of radical movements at the national political level depends on several factors. Some of these movements were so limited in their impact that they could be considered unsuccessful as a national political force. They grew as a protest against frustration but they did not have sufficient impact to provoke changes in the overall political system, because of repression or other limiting factors.

The peasant federation in the Convención valley in Peru was neutralized partly by having its demands acceded to and partly by severe measures of repression. The purpose of the movement, to bring about this radical change at the national level, was not achieved. This may be because the climax of a systematic campaign to escalate peasant action came at a moment when the peasantry in other areas of the country was not yet prepared to take over and spread the movement.

The growing bargaining power of the *Ligas Camponeses* in north-east Brazil provoked neutralizing efforts by more establishment-oriented unions created by the Church and later by the 'populist' government. As these unions, partly under the influence of the activities of leaders or former leaders of the *Ligas*, became more and more radical the whole system of new organizations was destroyed in a *coup d'état* in 1964. Only a skeleton of the former unions and federations was left.

## 2. SUCCESS AND NEUTRALIZATION OF PEASANT ORGANIZATIONS

The effects of the more successful radical peasant movements were usually limited, in the end, after a new, middle-sector elite had established itself in power with peasant support. The case of Mexico after 1940 demonstrates how strong peasant organizations can be neutralized and controlled by the over-all system, influenced by the traditional forces. During the Cárdenas regime of the late thirties, a monolithic peasant organization was created out of several regionally organized groups to form part of the overall political structure. Several strong militant groups were brought together in one organization, the Confederación Nacional Campesina, and thereby linked with the political system as a whole. After 1940 this structure was increasingly controlled by the 'middle sector', not identified with the peasants, but rather opposed to them. The bargaining power of the peasantry disappeared or was left unused. The main function of the official peasant organization, the CNC, was then to keep the peasants within the fold of the official party and mobilize support for the government at elections.

The relatively small 'middle sector', although larger than the traditional ruling class, reaped the benefits from modernization in Mexico, while the majority of the population, particularly the peasants, fell back into conditions not too different from those before the Revolution. New forms of 'internal colonialism' appeared. It should be noted that the reversal of the radical reformist policies after 1940 is partly (but only partly) a result of outside pressures, particularly from the USA which was interested in a politically stable Mexico in a period when fascist forces were becoming dangerously strong in their opposition to the radical experiments carried out during the Cárdenas regime. In the overall post-1940 context the CNC has lost its function as a promoter of a dynamic agrarian policy This is the main reason why considerable violence continues to prevail in the rural areas in Mexico and why, at times, radical movements occur which are repressed by army intervention. The assassination of the peasant leader Rubén Jaramillo in 1962, the massacre of peasants in Acapulco in 1967, the guerrilla forces in the highlands of Chihuahua in Madera and Guerrero (led until his death in 1972 by Genaro Vazquez), both still in operation, are symptoms of a potential for considerable unrest.

In Bolivia some of the same forces as in Mexico were at work, but had less impact because the post-revolutionary period was shorter, and because the revolutionary change in the rural areas was considerably more profound and immediate than in most of Mexico.

During the drive to organize the peasants and to distribute the land according to the law in Bolivia, there were few victims. Violence was largely avoided. This was partly due to the fact that the peasants were effectively armed. They could defend both themselves and those government functionaries who came to execute the laws in the few cases where landlords might have offered violent opposition. Special legislation was issued to regulate the rural security service which was in the hands of the peasants to guarantee a proper execution of the reform procedures. Peasants in Bolivia still keep much of their armed defence structure and have maintained the possibility of using their bargaining power to a much larger extent than in Mexico.

In Bolivia there is also a great deal more competition among the leadership, and the organization as a whole appears less monolithic than that of the Mexican CNC. The Bolivian CNTCB is also less solidly controlled by a firmly established political party, dominated by middle-sector interests. It must be kept in mind that there has not yet been an opportunity in Bolivia for a new type of commercial farmers' class to arise whose interests conflict with the peasants' as in Mexico. This is largely because commercial-scale farming is limited to the tropical lowlands, where agrarian reform has so far been marginal. Particularly at the local level, peasant unions play a more important role in Bolivia than in Mexico, and there is probably more active participation of the rank and file in the management of local and regional affairs, although in this area the degree of peasant participation still leaves much to be desired.

It should be noted that the peasant organization structure in Bolivia could possibly have been used to mobilize the peasantry behind a national development effort. Particularly after the radical land distribution, there was great enthusiasm among the peasants for new undertakings at all levels. It seems, however, that efforts were undertaken to calm and control this fervour rather than to channel it in effective ways. Many of the forces which try to prevent dynamic participation of the peasantry in the national economy could recover or remain in control.

Only one country, Cuba, has apparently been successful in giving the peasants a place in a new system which was the result of revolutionary change. It also has mobilized the peasantry effectively in a new development venture. New institutions have been fashioned in such a way as to keep the spirit of change and development alive among broad masses of the people.

Cuba before 1959 was already a country in which about sixty per cent of the population lived in urban areas and where the bargaining organizations of workers had gained considerable strength. This was also the case among the sugar-mill workers, but an estimated 500,000 farm labourers, including seasonal sugar-cane workers, were practically unorganized and lived under subsistence conditions. The sharecroppers and squatters and the 65,000 sugar-cane-growing tenants had hardly any organization and lived at the margin of society as a whole.

Active participation in the forces which brought a new regime to power in 1959 came from the poor peasants in the mountain region of the Sierra Maestra. Many of them were squatters who were continuously threatened by the large landowners and frequently evicted from the plots they tilled. It was in this area that already in 1958 a land reform programme was carried out, giving secure title to the squatters. After the Revolution, a sense of participation in a new national venture was created among the whole peasantry. Through the agrarian reform law of May 1959, more than 100,000 tenants, sharecroppers and squatters became owners of their plots, without any obligation to pay for the land. In addition to this land distribution, the agrarian reform programme transformed the large-scale enterprises, many of which were owned by foreign companies, into collective or state farms.

After the reform, about one third of those working in agriculture were small cultivators, working altogether forty-two per cent of all farm land. In this important sector, new institutions were also created. More than 150,000 small farmers were organized into local associations and cooperatives, which in 1961 were brought together into the National Association of Small Cultivators (ANAP). This association acts as an intermediary in the supply of credit in the scale of products at fair prices. ANAP has been particularly effective in channelling cheap credits (with four per cent interest) to the small farmers, in a system which gives over the supervisory task mainly to the local organization. Requests for credit are made to the Bank through a local cooperative organization which guides, approves and supervises the cultivation plan of each member. The available data do not indicate the extent to which the planning of the local organizations is integrated into the national plan.

In addition to organizing peasant participation in credit and other agricultural promotion efforts, ANAP forms part of a wider system of popular mobilization through the so-called mass organizations. These are associations for farmers, workers, women, students and other categories covering the whole country with an estimated direct participation of one out of every two adult Cubans. A special place is taken among the organizations by the Committees for the Defence of the Revolution (Comités de Defensa de la Revolución), which date from the period when the regime was threatened from various sides. They became multi-purpose citizens' groups used by the national leadership for recruiting support as well as promoting sanitation drives and other civic campaigns. Official reports claim that these committees have a membership of 1,500,000 persons, one out of every five Cubans, organized in a network of over 100,000 committees all over the country.

In addition to the new institutions, the mass communication media are amply used to keep a spirit of participation in a national 'struggle' alive among most of the population. The mass media, extensively spread in Cuba for many years, keep the people continuously informed about national problems and make an almost direct influence by the national leadership possible.

It would be highly useful if up-to-date studies of the mobilization of the peasantry and their participation in the national development effort in Cuba could be made. It seems clear that the main impulse for mobilization came from above, after the revolutionary government had come to power. Unlike Mexico and Bolivia, the peasant protest movement from below, although crucial in the initial stages of the guerrilla struggle in the Sierra Maestra, was not so large as to force the government to take the peasants into account once a new regime was established. However, the new government felt itself ideologically committed to a radical reform programme and mobilized the peasants, rather than neutralizing them as in Mexico and Bolivia. It possibly also felt the need for mass peasant support. It should be noted that the peasantry in Cuba was only a third of the population as a whole and not the overwhelming majority, as in the days of revolution and turmoil in Mexico and Bolivia.

## 3. THE CREATION OF ORGANIZATIONS FROM ABOVE: 'POPULISM'

In the light of the development of peasant organizations in Mexico and Bolivia it can be understood that other governments and parties have tried or are trying to create peasant organizations which are controlled by the overall political system from the outset. Peasant organizations stimulated from above receive benefits for their members before they have sufficient bargaining power to get such benefits on their own account.

Several Latin American governments have at some stage tried to mobilize the peasantry in a controlled way: Venezuela, Brazil (before 1964) and Guatemala (before 1954). However, this mobilization was carried out less whole-heartedly than in Mexico, Bolivia or Cuba, where peasants received arms to defend their interests and the regime that benefited them.* The governments of Venezuela, Brazil and Guatemala that promoted peasant mobilization could be considered 'populist'. Such regimes maintain that there is unity among the people, rather than a division (and struggle) along class lines. They try to content all classes. Mexico and Bolivia can also be considered 'populist' in this sense, particularly after a new equilibrium between different classes had been established.

Venezuela is apparently a case in point. The Federación Campesina de Venezuela was, from its foundation, dependent on the flow of certain benefits from the government to the peasants. Once a strong organization existed, and particularly after this organization had suffered several years of frustration under a repressive regime (1948–1958), the FCV reacted in a way not unlike the first peasant movements in Mexico and Bolivia. It displayed considerable political bargaining power through effective land invasions. But once the most militant groups were contented through land distribution, the FCV became a 'brokerage' system through which

---

* One can only speculate what would have happened to reform-oriented governments in Venezuela (1948), Guatemala (1954) and Brazil (1964), and the agrarian reform programme they were executing or initiating, had there been a loyal and powerfully organized peasantry to support them against the *coups* staged by the military.

benefits flowed to the peasant groups in exchange for their electoral support.

Only at one point did this system come close to running out of hand (with the invasions of 1958–60), and this was as a reaction to the fact that the military dictatorship in power for ten years had come to repress even this well-controlled political patronage system. It is clear that one of the most important factors that keeps this system functioning with some degree of effectiveness in Venezuela is the availability of considerable financial resources, coming from oil revenues. These resources made it possible to overcome the landlords' opposition in the first place; then the peasantry could be kept in expectation of benefits by a careful and strategic distribution of benefits in those areas where dissidence might develop. It should also be noted that Venezuela, like Cuba, is different from many other Latin American countries in that its rural population represents only about one third of the total.

In Brazil a similar approach was tried in 1963–4 when the government created a national system of peasant organizations in order to guarantee electoral support and to overshadow the Peasant Leagues and other militant peasant organizations that existed in some regions. However, through elections within the unions, the new structure soon came under the control of their most radical elements, which was probably one of the reasons why the traditional elites and the army eliminated the whole political system in 1964.

A similar thing had happened ten years before in Guatemala in the counter-reform of 1954. However, the process of repression after a more or less controlled peasant mobilization had taken place led to an awakening of the peasants to their interests as a class in the same way as happened as a result of the *violencia* in Colombia (and as could possibly happen in Brazil).

It is clear from the Guatemalan case, and even clearer from

the Venezuelan (1948–58) and Bolivian (1946–52) cases, that severe repression after a period of a 'populist' regime (which gives certain benefits and hopes to the peasantry) creates a climate favourable to radical peasant movements. Such movements can then be contained only by considerable concessions, if not overall reform or revolution favourable to the peasants. The conservative reaction of the traditional elites to the moderate reforms of the more or less 'populist' regimes of Villarroel in Bolivia (1943–6) and of Betancourt in Venezuela (1945–8) created the conditions for the rise of radical peasant movements that came close to being revolutionary in 1952 and 1958 respectively.

In Guatemala a similar development can at present be halted only by a considerable show of force and repression. A great number of peasants and peasant leaders have been assassinated between 1962 and the present day without ending the unrest prevailing in the rural areas. One could say that the intransigent reaction of the landed elite, in repressing peasant organizations even when they were stimulated from above by a reformist government, has brought a higher degree of 'class consciousness' to the peasants.

'Populist' governments such as existed in Brazil before 1964 and Guatemala before 1954 may create vertically controlled peasant organizations, but the struggle in which these organizations unavoidably get involved once they defend peasant interests brings a greater solidarity and 'class consciousness' to increasingly large sections of the peasantry. This is not a natural growth phenomenon, but a result of the intransigent reaction of those whose interests are opposed to the peasants. How the 'populist' system will develop depends mainly, it seems, on the willingness of the traditional elite to give in to legitimate demands and to conform to the need for radical change. If they resist the pressures from the peasants, as they mostly do, the peasants will radicalize and escalate their demands and tactics of struggle. The peaceful coexistence of various classes within the 'populist' system will then collapse. Repression of the peasants follows, but this makes clear to them where their basic interests lie, and the chances that they will be controlled again, without repression, appear small. Guatemala, where the peasantry was isolated and had a highly traditional way of life, is a case in point. There are many indications that the conditions for a mobilization of the indigenous peasants for radical, reformist, or revolutionary action are better than ever in that country. This is quite understandable after the developments described above. Particularly important is the fact that 'populist' governments stimulate a high level of expectation, but are unable to realize the promises, because of the unwillingness and resistance of the traditional elite to adapt to new situations. Frustration, radicalization and repression leading to greater radicalization seem to be a recurrent theme in present Latin American peasant politics.

## 4. OTHER FACTORS PROMOTING REVOLUTIONARY POTENTIAL

For those who see in revolutionary changes of the Latin American societies the only way to dynamic development, the present tendencies in the rural areas seem in the long run to offer good chances. As was noted in the Survey of the Alliance for Progress, *Insurgency in Latin America* : *

There exists an ideologically unfocused quasi-insurgency of peasant uprisings as one aspect of the violence that is an endemic feature of political life in many Latin American countries. Usually these have sought a remedy for a specific grievance or have been the attempt of land squatters to protect their claims against the government forces. This shades into rural banditry.

* Committee on Foreign Relations, United States Senate, Washington, D.C., 15 January 1968, doc. 86–406, p. 8.

Peasant-connected incidents of this type are not insurgency but can develop into it. Legitimate guerrillas often utilize peasant unrest or incorporate rural bandits into their ranks.

Ironically enough, this observation was made in the context of a top-level debate on the foreign policy of the USA. It is well known, and at times recognized, that this policy has tried to make impossible consistent 'populist' reforms in several Latin American countries where US interests have been at stake. The 'counter-reform' in Guatemala in 1954 is the most renowned case. In several countries such as Mexico (where during 1934–40 many US estates were expropriated) or Bolivia (where few US landed interests existed) 'populist' governments were left alone to carry out land reforms. Although the subject has hardly been studied systematically, there is some evidence that the US favoured the neutralization of the peasantry and the de-emphasis on land reform during the post-1940 governments in Mexico, particularly during the term of president Miguel Alemán (1946–52). In Bolivia, USAID community development advisers were influential in neutralizing to some extent the peasant syndicate structure by creating parallel community councils for the promotion of community projects, rather than relying on the existing peasant unions. Only in Cuba, where US influence, after it had tried to subvert or overthrow the revolutionary government, was completely cut off, could a consistent mobilization of the peasantry and their participation in a national development effort be achieved. US policies have not always been consistent. While in the early sixties the Declaration of Punta del Este emphasized the need for agrarian reform as a precondition for overall development in Latin America and for receiving US aid, several governments which allowed forces to develop that might be helpful in the promulgation or carrying out of effective land reform, such as the Goulart regime in Brazil in 1964, were overthrown with the tacit or active support of the US.

US aid to peasant organizations is generally channelled only for those movements that do not strongly emphasize the need for radical land reform. In some cases, however, such as Venezuela in the early sixties, land reform and peasant organization was strongly supported because it helped to prevent what was called 'Castro's attempts at insurgency'.

The extent to which 'populist' governments are liable to foreign pressure depends on the type of foreign interests involved, which varies from country to country. At the US policy level, one increasingly hears voices that denounce the rigidly anti-reformist US pressures of the last few years, particularly the various forms of 'military aid' given to Latin American governments. However, the tendency to defend 'stability' at all costs, rather than to allow significant reforms to occur, seems to continue. In the long run this policy, emphasizing economic 'development' without social reform, may enhance the 'revolutionary potential' of the peasantry even more than the 'populist' reform policies.

It is not only the 'populist' regimes that create instability and frustration among the peasantry. Almost any development policy has this effect since it upsets the *status quo* and often leads to frustration rather than improvement. The Colombian land reform programme, emphasizing technical improvements and infrastructure building, can be considered typical of the half-hearted development effort that creates frustration among the peasants. INCORA's programme was often propagandized as *the* example of the new Alliance for Progress reform strategy. The failure of this programme to bring about any significant social reform has been recognized. As a result continuous peasant unrest is a characteristic of Colombian rural life.

Wherever new and modernizing influences enter into the rural areas, frustration makes its appearance. This is often an unplanned result of a variety of development projects and programmes, including irrigation schemes, settlement projects, community development efforts, that are increasingly undertaken in Latin America. The traditional *status quo* is changed in such cases mostly in ways which give little participation to the peasantry. Frequently the established elite or a privileged minority gets such a large share of the benefits that a development programme loses its appeal for the peasants. In addition there are often directly opposing traditional interests which hinder any programme that might lead to effective social change at the local level.

In the first chapters of this book it was demonstrated that the peasants' commonly shown distrust of local development projects is not so much an irrational aspect of traditional peasant behaviour as an awareness of the severe limitations of such projects, which basically cover up unbearable conditions rather than bring improvement. Through effective involvement in such projects, in rural areas in Central America and in Chile, I was able to learn gradually that this peasant distrust is quite rational and justified and that if properly utilized it can be a condition for effective and militant peasant organization. Distrust is a logical reaction of the peasant to the 'resistance to change' of the landed elite.

Ironically, it appears that it is precisely landlord opposition and the resulting frustration among the peasants that is one of the main factors leading to the emergence of radical movements which cannot be contented until really significant reforms have been brought about. While the short-term effect of many community projects, such as the one in which I participated in El Salvador, seems to be increasing frustration, in the long run such effort may thus have the positive effect of enhancing the 'organizability' of the peasants. The more radical leaders of newly created organizations that appeal to the most basic and strongly felt needs of the peasantry, including the desire for basic structural reforms, will increasingly find response, as was the case in the Punitaqui project in Chile that I assisted.

In the rural areas where some form of half-hearted change or development takes place, frustration will grow and so will the likelihood of protest, civil disobedience, or even civil violence. This fact, occurring with increasing frequency in Latin American countries, conforms to a general trend: the more expectations are aroused and, relatively, frustrated, the more the apathy and tradition-bound conformity which has dominated the rural areas for centuries will make way for an aggressive attitude.

The approach of those traditional groups that try to avoid any change at all in order to maintain their privileged position is understandable, but the prevention of change is now becoming more and more impossible in Latin American countries. Even in isolated regions there are modernizing influences. Roads, schools, teachers, transistor radios, villagers who have worked in urban areas or mines and return to their birthplace, are all factors which begin the erosion of the *status quo*. The state of violence, inherent in a society with a rigid social structure that divides the population into a few holders of power and a majority which has little or no share in economic benefits and political power, becomes increasingly unbearable after modernizing changes occur. Turning the clock back after certain changes favourable to the peasants have been made can be achieved by increasing repression, but seems to have a radicalizing effect in the long run.

Whether the increasingly favourable climate for militant peasant movements will be utilized depends to a large extent on the willingness of urban allies to support and guide the peasant organizations. Since the forces that oppose representative peasant organizations, the traditional landed elite, are highly sophisticated and do not hesitate to use any possible means to block the peasant pressures that emerge, it is logical that the peasants need allies of equal sophistication to help defend their legitimate interests. Practically all cases of peasant movements known to be strong have had such allies.

In this respect it is important to see that an erosion of the *status quo* is also taking place within the traditional elite itself. There seems to be an increasing number of sons of the wealthier classes, including the landed elite, who rather than inheriting status and wealth from their forefathers want to build a career and serve their country through ways which refute their background. Some of them become advisers to popular pressure groups, others use even more risky and spectacular approaches and join movements of armed resistance against the established order. As a result of the latter some of the most backward areas of Peru and Guatemala have been, or are being, opened up through military–civic action programmes which entered those regions in order to eliminate foci of guerrillas operating there. These forces of modernization appear to bring about the 'erosion of the *status quo*' in areas where the forces of population increase, urban contacts and consequences of natural erosion are not yet strongly felt.

For revolutionary movements of the past similar phenomena have been noted. These forces are at present working with increasing strength in Latin America. Fidel Castro, Francisco Julião, and Hugo Blanco are examples of popular leaders who were by birth members of elite classes. Part of the strategy for promoting peasant organization might be directed towards increasing the number of dissidents among the traditional elites. As we have seen, some of the younger members of the traditional elites seem to be willing and eager to accept new constructive roles in which they can find self-esteem and status and which are more in step with the development needs of their countries than the traditional roles of their fathers. One could imagine that many young members of the traditional elite feel that self-esteem derived from personal effort and capacity in the fulfilment of such new roles is potentially more satisfactory than status derived from inheritance and the copying of outdated patterns of seignorial life. As yet few systematic efforts have been made to tap the potentialities of these youths.

It seems that the restlessness of youth and student groups in many countries is not unrelated to an attitude of protest against the traditional value-system which upholds the overall *status quo*, most sharply visible in the rural areas. A factor of great importance in this respect is that it becomes increasingly clear that the most conservative and repressive governments in Latin America are supported in the name of 'stability' by foreign influences, particularly the USA. Especially in those foreign countries where agrarian reform and peasant organization efforts or plans were frustrated, for example Guatemala in 1954 and Brazil in 1964, such outside interventions were more or less obvious, but they are increasingly recognized in many other countries. In academic circles in Latin America criticism of US intervention and economic domination has become a rallying point for protest action, but as yet few links have been made between these intellectual protests and the actual or potential peasant resistance. The few guerrilla groups which have operated in some Latin American countries seem on the whole to have failed to make proper contact with the peasantry and to convince them that their causes coincided. There is a considerable gap between the urban intellectuals, the defecting young members of the upper classes and students on the one hand, and the distrustful peasantry on the other. One proof of this gap seems to be the expectation that once a group starts to organize a focus of revolutionary resistance to the overall system in some region the peasantry will follow the call for revolt without much preparation and without going through several stages of 'conscientization' and organization. That the establishment of a close link and collaboration between urban political forces, engaged in the creation of radical change, and the peasantry and its natural leaders is feasible is demonstrated by the examples in this book.

Up to the present few programmes exist where university students have been stimulated on a large scale to participate actively in rural organization efforts. However, where this has been done, some groups of young people of the educated classes have responded enthusiastically and shown ability to establish relationships with the peasantry which differ from the traditional pattern. The Promoción Popular Universitaria in Peru and some university-sponsored rural promotion programmes in Chile are interesting examples. The first was practically discontinued because of its renovating or even radicalizing impact, particularly among the students.

Another group that has drawn attention to itself as a powerful potential ally of the peasants are the local priests who have been influenced by new social teachings currently becoming important. Several groups of priests, interested and actively engaged in work in this field, have been formed in Colombia and Peru. The fact that students as well as priests belong to a kind of institution (university and church respectively) that can be made independent of the overall traditionally controlled system could be an advantage. Altogether, it seems that a broad field for experimentation in peasant organization lies open.

How 'revolutionary' future peasant movements will be seems to depend largely on the measures of intransigence of the traditional 'elites' and the national and international forces that support them. From past experience it is clear that the more resistant the Latin American elites are to change, the more radical the demands of the peasantry – and their means of struggle – will become.

# Bibliography

For an extensive general bibliography on peasant movements and organizations in Latin America, see Gerrit Huizer and Cynthia N. Hewitt, 'Bibliography on Peasant Movements', in Henry A. Landsberger (ed.), *Latin American Peasant Movements*, Cornell University Press, 1969.

See also the bibliography in the original unabridged version of this book, Gerrit Huizer, *The Revolutionary Potential of Peasants in Latin America*, Lexington, Mass.: Heath Lexington Books, 1972, pp. 229–37, where a list of the author's articles on matters covered in this book is included.

The bibliography of the most important literature used in this study is as follows:

Adams, Richard N., 'Rural Labor', in John J. Johnson (ed.), *Continuity and Change in Latin America*, Stanford University Press, 1964, pp. 49–78.

Adams, Richard N., 'Social Change in Guatemala and US Policy' in Richard N. Adams *et al.*, *Social Change in Latin America Today*, Council of Foreign Relations, New York, 1961.

Adler, Judith, *The Politics of Land Reform in Mexico: The Case of La Comarca Lagunera*, M.Phil. Thesis, London School of Economics, 1970.

Aguirre, Beltrán Gonzalo, *Regiones de Refugio: El Desarrollo de la Comunidad y el Proceso Dominical en Mestizo America*, Instituto Indigenista Interamericano, Mexico D.F., 1967.

Alexander, Robert J., *The Bolivian National Revolution*, Rutgers University Press, 1958.

Alexander, Robert J., *Organized Labor in Latin America*, Free Press, New York, 1965.

Anderson, Charles W., 'Reform-mongering and the Uses of Political Power', *Inter-American Economic Affairs*, Vol. 19, No. 2, Autumn 1965.

Anderson, Charles W., *Toward a Theory of Latin American Politics*, LTC Reprint No. 10, Land Tenure Center, University of Wisconsin, 1964.

Antezana, Luis, *Bosquejo Histórico del Movimiento Sindical Campesino en Bolivia*, La Paz, Bolivia, Agosto 1968, mimeo.

Antezana, Luis, *El Movimiento Obrero Boliviano (1935–1943)*, La Paz, Bolivia, 1966.

Antezana, Luis, y Romero Hugo, *Origen, Desarrollo y Situación Actual del Sindicalismo Campesino en Bolivia*, CIDA–LTC, La Paz, 1968, mimeo.

Banfield, Edward C., *The Moral Basis of Backward Society*, Free Press of Glencoe, New York, 1958.

Barraclough, Solon, and Domike, Arthur, 'Agrarian Structure in Seven Latin American Countries', *Land Economics*, Vol. XLII, No. 4, November 1966, LTC Reprint No. 25, Land Tenure Center, University of Wisconsin.

Blanco, Hugo, *El Camino de Nuestra Revolución*, Ediciones Revolución Peruana, Lima, 1964.

Blok, Anton, 'Mafia and Peasant Rebellion as Contrasting Factors in Sicilian Latifundism', *European Journal of Sociology*, Vol. X, 1969.

Boissevain, Jeremy, 'Patronage in Sicily', *Man*, Vol. 1, No. 1, March 1966.

Bourricaud, François, *Cambios en Puno*, Instituto Indigenista Interamericano, Ediciones Especiales, No. 48, Mexico, 1967.

Brandenburg, Frank, *The Making of Modern Mexico*, Prentice-Hall, Englewood Cliffs, N.J., 1964.

Camargo, Procopio, *O Movimiento do Natal*, Centre de Documentation sur l'Action des Eglises dans le Monde, Brussels, 1968.

Carroll, Thomas F., 'Land Reform as an Explosive Force in Latin

America', in J. J. TePaske and S. N. Fisher (eds.), *Explosive Forces in Latin America*, Ohio University Press, 1964.

Carroll, Thomas F., 'The Land Reform Issue in Latin America', in Albert O. Hirschman (ed.), *Latin American Issues, Essays and Comments*, The Twentieth Century Fund, New York, 1961.

Castillo, Carlos Manuel, 'La Economía Agrícola en la Región del Bajío', *Problemas Agrícolas e Industriales de México*, Vol. VIII, Nos. 3–4.

Chaplin, David, 'Peru's Postponed Revolution', *World Politics*, Vol. XX, No. 3, April 1968.

Chevalier, François, 'Ejido y Estabilidad en México', *América Indígena*, Vol. XXVII, No. 2, Mexico D.F., April 1967.

Chevalier, François, 'Un Factor Decisivo de la Revolución Agraria de Mexico : El Levantamiento de Zapata (1911–1919)', *Cuadernos Americanos*, Vol. XIX, No. 6, November–December 1960.

CIDA, Brazil, *Land Tenure Conditions and Socio-Economic Development of the Agricultural Sector*, Union Panamericana, Washington. D.C., 1966.

CIDA, Colombia, *Tenencia de la Tierra y Desarrollo Socio-Económico del Sector Agrícola*, Union Panamericana, Washington. D.C., 1966.

CIDA, Guatemala, *Tenencia de la Tierra y Desarrollo Socio-Económico del Sector Agrícola*, Union Panamericana, Washington. D.C., 1965.

CIDA, Perú, *Tenencia de la Tierra y Desarrollo Socio-Económico del Sector Agrícola*, Union Panamericana, Washington. D.C., 1966.

Condarco, Morales Ramiro, Zárate, *El 'Temible' Willka*, História de la Rebelión Indígena de 1899, La Paz, Bolivia, 1966.

Correia de Andrade, Manoel, *A Terra e Homen no Nordeste*, Editora Brasiliense, São Paulo, 1963.

Coser, Lewis A., *Continuities in the Study of Social Conflict*, Free Press, New York, 1968.

Coser, Lewis A., *The Functions of Social Conflict*, Glencoe : Free Press, 1956.

Craig, Wesley W., 'The Peasant Movement of La Convención, Peru : Dynamics of Rural Labor Organization', in Henry A.

Landsberger (ed.), *Latin American Peasant Movements*, Cornell University Press, 1969.

Dandler, Hanhart Jorge, *Local Group, Community, and Nation: A Study of Changing Structure in Ucureña, Bolivia (1935–1952)*, M.A. Thesis, University of Wisconsin, 1967, mimeo.

Delgado, Oscar, *Reforma Agraria y Desarrollo Rural en una Area del Altiplano Norte de Bolivia*, CIDA–LTC, Estudio de Caso, 1968, mimeo.

Delgado, Oscar (ed.), *Reformas agrarias en América Latina: Procesos y perspectivas*, Fondo de Cultura Económica, Mexico, 1965.

Dew, Edward, *Politics in the Altiplano: The Dynamics of Change in Rural Peru*, University of Texas Press, 1969.

Dolci, Danilo, *Waste*, MacGibbon and Kee, London, 1963.

Duran, Marco Antonio, *El Agrarismo Mexicano*, Siglo Veintiuno Editores, Mexico D.F., 1967.

Eckstein, Salomón, *El Ejido Colectivo en México*, Fondo de Cultura Económica, Mexico, 1966.

Erasmus, Charles J., 'Community Development and the Encogido Syndrome', *Human Organization*, Vol. 27, No. 1, Spring 1968.

Erasmus, Charles J., *Man Takes Control: Cultural Development and American Aid*, University of Minnesota Press, 1961.

Erasmus, Charles J., 'Upper Limits of Peasantry and Agrarian Reform: Bolivia, Venezuela and Mexico Compared', *Ethnology*, Vol. 6, January 1967.

Facó, Rui, *Cangaceiros e Fanáticos*, Editora Civilização Brasileira, Rio de Janeiro, 1965.

Fals Borda, Orlando, *Campesinos de los Andes: Estudio Sociológico de Saucio*, Bogotá, 1961.

Feder, Ernest, 'Societal Opposition to Peasant Movements and its Effect on Farm People in Latin America', in Henry A. Landsberger (ed.), *Latin American Peasant Movements*, Cornell University Press, 1969.

Flores, Edmundo, 'Land Reform in Bolivia', *Land Economics*, Vol. XXX, No. 2, May 1954.

Flores, Edmundo, *Tratado de Economía Agrícola*, Fondo de Cultura Económica, Mexico D.F., 1961.

Foster, George M., *Empire's Children: The People of Tzintzun- tzan*, Smithsonian Institution, Institute of Social Anthropology, Washington. D.C., Publ. No: 6, 1948.

Foster, George M., 'Peasant Society and the Image of Limited Good', *American Anthropologist*, Vol. 67, No. 2, April 1965, p. 303.

Friedrich, Paul, 'A Mexican Cacicazgo', *Ethnology*, Vol. IV, No. 2, April 1965.

Galjart, Benno, 'Class and "Following" in Rural Brazil', *América Latina*, Vol. 7, No. 3, 1964.

Galjart, Benno, *Itaguaí; Old Habits and New Practices in a Brazi- lian Land Settlement*, Wageningen, 1968.

Galjart, Benno, 'Old Patrons and New', *Sociologia Ruralis*, Vol. VII, No. 4, 1967.

Gilly, Adolfo, 'The Guerilla Movement in Guatemala', *Monthly Review*, Vol. 17, Nos. 1 and 2, May and June 1965.

Goldrich, Daniel, 'Toward Comparative Politicization in Latin America', in Dwight B. Heath and Richard N. Adams (eds.), *Contemporary Cultures and Societies of Latin America*, Random House, New York, 1965.

González Casanova, Pablo, *La Democracia en México*, Ediciones E R A, Segunda Edición, Mexico D.F., 1967.

González Ramírez, Manuel, *La Revolución Social de México*, Vol. III, *El Problema Agrario*, Fondo de Cultura Económica, Mexico D.F., 1966.

Gruening, Ernest, *Mexico and its Heritage*, New York, 1928.

Gurr, Ted, 'Psychological Factors in Civil Violence', *World Politics, A Quarterly Journal of International Relations*, Vol. XX, No. 2, January 1968.

Gutiérrez, José, *La Rebeldía Colombiana, Observaciones Psico- lógicas sobre la Actualidad Política*, Ediciones Tercer Mundo, Bogotá, 1962.

Guzmán Campos, German, *La Violencia en Colombia*, Parte De- scriptiva, Ediciones Progreso, Cali., 1968.

Heath, Dwight B., 'The Aymara Indians and Bolivia's Revolu- tion', *Inter-American Economic Affairs*, Vol. 19, No. 4, Spring 1966.

Heath, Dwight B., Erasmus, Charles J., and Buechler, Hans C.,

*Land Reform and Social Revolution in Bolivia*, Land Tenure Center, University of Wisconsin, 1965, mimeo.

Hewitt, Cynthia N., 'An Analysis of the Peasant Movement of Pernambuco, Brazil: 1961–1964', in Henry A. Landsberger (ed.), *Latin American Peasant Movements*, Cornell University Press, 1972.

Hirschman, Albert O., *Journeys towards Progress: Studies of Economic Policy-making in Latin America*, Twentieth Century Fund, New York, 1963.

Hobsbawm, Eric J., *Problèmes agraires à La Convención (Pérou)*, communication présentée au Colloque International CNRS sur Les Problèmes Agraires en Amérique Latine, Paris, 11–16 October 1965.

Holmberg, Allan R., 'Changing Community Attitudes and Values in Peru: A Case Study in Guided Change', in Richard N. Adams *et al.*, *Social Change in Latin America Today*, Council of Foreign Relations, New York, 1961.

Holmberg, Allan R., 'Land Tenure and Planned Social Change: A Case from Vicos, Peru', *Human Organization*, Vol. 18, No. 1, 1959, p. 9.

Horowitz, Irving Louis, 'Party Charisma', *Studies in Comparative International Development*, Vol. I, No. 7, 1965.

International Labour Office, *Freedom of Association and Conditions of Work in Venezuela*, Studies and Reports, New Series, No. 21, Geneva, 1950.

International Labour Office, *Indigenous Peoples*, Studies and Reports, New Series, No. 35, Geneva, 1953.

International Labour Office, *The Landless Farmer in Latin America*, Studies and Reports, New Series, No. 47, Geneva, 1957.

Julião, Francisco, *Brazil: Antes y Después*, Editorial Neustro Tiempo, Mexico, 1968.

Julião, Francisco, *Escucha Campesino*, introducción de Edgardo Carvalho, Ediciones Presente, Montevideo, 1962.

Julião, Francisco (in co-authorship with Clodomir Santos de Morais), *Que son las Ligas Campesinas?*, Ediciones ARCA, Montevideo, 1963.

Kadt, Emanuel de, 'Religion, the Church and Social Change in

Brazil', in Claudio Veliz (ed.), *The Politics of Conformity in Latin America*, Oxford University Press, London, 1967.

Landsberger, Henry A., 'The Role of Peasant Movements and Revolts in Development: An Analytical Framework', *Bulletin, International Institute for Labour Studies*, No. 4, February 1968.

Landsberger, Henry A., and Hewitt, Cynthia N., *Preliminary Report on a Case Study of Mexican Peasant Organizations*, Cornell University, mimeo.

Landsberger, Henry A., and Hewitt, Cynthia N., *Ten Sources of Weakness and Cleavage in Latin American Peasant Movements*, paper read at the Second International Congress of Rural Sociology, Enschede, Netherlands, 5–10 August 1968.

Letts, Ricardo C., 'Breve Historia Contemporanea de la Lucha por la Reforma Agraria en el Perú', *Economia y Agricultura*, Vol. I, No. 2, Lima, 1963–4.

Lewis, Oscar, *Life in a Mexican Village: Tepoztlán Restudied*, University of Illinois Press, 1963.

Liga de Agrónomos Socialistas, *La Comarca Lagunera, El Colectivismo Agrario en México*, Publ. No. 15, Mexico, 1940.

Loomis, Charles P., *et al.*, *Turrialba: Social Systems and the Introduction of Change*. Glencoe: Free Press, 1953.

Lord, Peter P., *The Peasantry as an Emerging Political Factor in Mexico, Bolivia and Venezuela*, LTC Paper No. 35, Land Tenure Center, University of Wisconsin, 1965.

MacLean y Estenos, Roberto, *La Reforma Agraria en el Perú*, Cuadernos de Sociología, Instituto de Investigaciones Sociales, UNAM, Mexico D.F., 1965.

MacLean y Estenos, Roberto, 'La Revolución de 1910 y el Problema Agrario de México', *Estudios Sociológicos*, Tomo II, IX Congreso Nacional de Sociología, Mexico, 1958.

Magaña, Gildardo, *Emiliano Zapata y el Agrarismo en México*, Editorial Ruto México, 1951, 5 tomos.

Malpica, Mario A., *Biografía de la Revolución*, Ediciones Ensayos Sociales, Lima, 1967.

Martínez Mugica, Apolinar, *Primo Tapia, Semblanza de un Revolucionario Michoacano*, 2nd ed., Mexico, 1946.

Melville, Thomas and Margie, *Guatemala – Another Vietnam?*, Penguin Books, 1971.

Mendieta y Nuñez, Lucio, *El Problema Agrario de México*, 7th ed., Editorial Porrua, Mexico, 1959.

Nathan, Paul, 'México en la Epoca de Cárdenas', *Problemas Agrícolas e Industriales de México*, Vol. VII, No. 3, Mexico, 1955.

Neira, Hugo, *Cuzco: Tierra y Muerte, Reportaje al Sur*, Editorial Problemas de Hoy, Lima, 1964.

Newbold, Stokes, 'Receptivity of Communist Fomented Agitation in Rural Guatemala', *Economic Development and Cultural Change*, Vol. 5, No. 4, 1957.

Padgett, L. Vincent, *The Mexican Political System*, Houghton Mifflin, Boston, 1966.

Patch, Richard W., 'Bolivia: U.S. Assistance in a Revolutionary Setting', in Richard N. Adams et al., *Social Change in Latin America Today*, Council of Foreign Relations, New York, 1961.

Patch, Richard W., *Freedom and Development, Rural Decision-Making and Agricultural Development*, LTC Paper No. 22, Land Tenure Center, University of Wisconsin, July 1966, mimeo.

Paulson, Belden H., 'Difficulties and Prospects for Community Development in North-East Brazil', *Inter-American Economic Affairs*, Vol. 17, No. 4, Spring 1964.

Paulson, Belden H., *Local Political Patterns in North-East Brazil: A Community Case Study*, Land Tenure Center, University of Wisconsin, August 1964, mimeo.

Payne, James L., *Labor and Politics in Peru: The System of Political Bargaining*, Yale University Press, 1965.

Pearson, Neale J., 'Latin American Peasant Pressure Groups and the Modernization Process', *Journal of International Affairs*, Vol. XX, No. 2, 1966.

Pearson, Neale J., 'The Peasant Movement in Guatemala, 1944-1954', in Henry A. Landsberger (ed.), *Latin American Peasant Movements*, Cornell University Press, 1969.

Petras, James, and Zeitlin, Maurice, 'Miners and Agrarian Radicalism', in James Petras and Maurice Zeitlin (eds.), *Latin America: Reform or Revolution?*, Fawcett Premier Books, 1968.

Powell, John D., *The Politics of Agrarian Reform in Venezuela: History, System and Process*, Ph.D. Thesis (Pol Sc.), University of Wisconsin, 1966, mimeo.

Powell, John D., *Preliminary Report on the Federación Campesina de Venezuela: Origins, Organization, Leadership and Role in the Agrarian Reform Program*, Research Paper Land Tenure Center, University of Wisconsin, No. 9, September 1964, mimeo.

Powell, John D., *The Role of the Federación Campesina de Venezuela and Related Political Aspects*, manuscript prepared for CIDA study, 1967.

Powell, John D., 'The Peasant Movement in Venezuela', in Henry A. Landsberger (ed.), *Latin American Peasant Movements*, Cornell University Press, 1969.

Prebisch, Raul, *Towards a Dynamic Development Policy for Latin America*, United Nations, ECLA, E/CN. 12/680, 1963, mimeo.

Quijada, Ramón, *Reforma Agraria en Venezuela*, Editorial Arte, Caracas, 1963.

Quijano Obregón, Aníbal, 'Contemporary Peasant Movements', in Seymour Martin Lipset and Aldo Solari (eds.), *Elites in Latin America*, Oxford University Press, New York, 1967.

Quijano Obregón, Aníbal, 'El Movimiento Campesino del Perú y sus Líderes', *América Latina*, Vol. VIII, No. 4, 1965.

Santos de Morais, Clodomir, *Comportamiento Ideológico de las Clases y Capas del Campo en el Proceso de Organización*, ICIRA, Santiago, Chile, 1965, mimeo.

Schmitt, Karl M., *Communism in Mexico: A Study in Political Frustration*, University of Texas Press, 1965.

Scott, Robert E., *Mexican Government in Transition*, University of Illinois Press, revised edition, 1964.

Senior, Clarence, *Land Reform and Democracy*, University of Florida Press, 1958.

Silva Herzog, Jesús, *El Agrarismo Mexicano y la Reforma Agraria*, Fondo de Cultura Económica, Mexico, 1959.

Simpson, Eyler N., *The Ejido: Mexico's Way Out*, University of North Carolina Press, 1937.

Stavenhagen, Rodolfo, 'Clases, Colonialismo y Aculturación', *América Latina*, Vol. VI, No. 4, 1963.

Stavenhagen, Rodolfo (ed.), *Agrarian Problems and Peasant Movements in Latin America*, Anchor Books, New York, 1970.

Survey of the Alliance for Progress, *Colombia – A Case History of USAID*, Committee on Foreign Relations, US Senate, Doc. 21–145, Washington. D.C., 1969.

Survey of the Alliance for Progress, *Insurgency in Latin America*, Committee on Foreign Relations, US Senate, Doc. 86–406, Washington. D.C., 1968.

Survey of the Alliance for Progress, *Labor Policies and Programs*, Committee on Foreign Relations, US Senate, Doc. 87–782, Washington. D.C., 1968.

Tannenbaum, Frank, *The Mexican Agrarian Revolution*, Macmillan, New York, 1929.

Tannenbaum, Frank, *Peace by Revolution: Mexico after 1910*, Columbia University Press, 1933, paperback edition 1966.

Thiesenhusen, William C., 'Grassroots Economic Pressures in Chile: An Enigma for Development Planners', *Economic Development and Cultural Change*, April 1968.

Torres Restrepo, Camilo, *La Violencia y los Cambios Socioculturales en las Areas Rurales Colombianas*, Memoria del Primer Congreso Nacional de Sociología, Bogotá, 1963.

Vazquez, Mario C., *Hacienda, Peonaje y Servidumbre en los Andes Peruanos*, Monografías Andinas, No. 1, Editorial Estudios Andinos, Lima, 1961.

Villaneuva, Victor, *Hugo Blanco y la Rebelión Campesina*, Editorial Juan Mejía Baca, Lima, 1967.

Wertheim, W. F., *East-West Parallels*, Van Hoeve, The Hague, 1964.

Wertheim, W. F., 'Sociology between Yesterday and Tomorrow', *Comparative Studies in Society and History*, Vol. IX, No. 2, January 1967.

Weyl, Nathaniel and Sylvia, *The Reconquest of Mexico: The Years of Lázaro Cárdenas*, Oxford University Press, London, 1939.

Whetten, Nathan L., *Guatemala, the Land and the People*, Yale University Press, 1961.

Whetten, Nathan L., *Rural Mexico*, University of Chicago Press, 1948.

Wilkie, Mary E., *A Report on Rural Syndicates in Pernambuco, Brazil*, revised version, M.A. Thesis, University of Wisconsin, 1967.

Wolf, Eric R., 'Aspects of Group Relations in a Complex Society: Mexico', *American Anthropologist*, Vol. 58, No. 6, 1956.

# Acknowledgement

Since I was working with various agencies of the United Nations while the material for this book was collected I am heavily indebted to these agencies, particularly I.L.O., for the possibilities they gave me to work on the subjects covered by this book. Opinions expressed are of course my own responsibility. I am also greatly indebted to many friends and colleagues who have given me their advice and support. Amongst them I want to mention : Judith Adler, Desmond Anker, Luis Antezana, Solon Barraclouch, Anton Blok, Jeremy Boissevain, Thomas Carroll, Arthur Domike, Ernest Feder, German Guzman Campos, Andrew Gunder Frank, Benno Galjart, Horacio Labastida, Henry Landsberger, Clodomir Santos de Morais, John Powell, Anibal Quijano, Rodolfo Stavenhagen, Marvin Sternberg and last but not least Wim Wertheim, who supervised the original unabridged version of this book as a Ph.D. dissertation.

I want to dedicate this book to Guadalupe Campos of village San Luis, El Salvador and many other peasants whose distrust and friendship taught me about the dignity and revolutionary potential of the repressed.

# Index

# Political Leaders of Latin America

*Richard Bourne*

Latin American politics are of increasing importance in world affairs. This volume contains portraits of six political leaders of the region : individually they stress the diversity that lies between caudillo and Communist; together they may be taken to typify the face of Latin American government and the special problems confronting it.

| | |
|---|---|
| Che Guevara | The Argentinian revolutionary who conquered in Cuba and died in Bolivia |
| Eduardo Frei | The President of Chile and the first Christian-Democratic president in Latin America |
| Alfredo Stroessner | The Army dictator of Paraguay |
| Juscelino Kubitschek | The President of Brazil from 1956 to 1960 and founder of Brasilia |
| Carlos Lacerda | who has helped to overthrow three Brazilian presidents |
| Evita Perón | The glamorous wife of the Argentinian dictator who combined military and labour supporters in a powerful nationalist movement |